Squib-Kick It to a Fat Guy . . .

Squib-Kick It to a Fat Guy ...

and 699 more memorable quotes from the playbook of Coach Mike Leach

Alan Burton

Anarene Books

Cover and inside photos provided by Washington State University Athletic Communications.

Author photo provided by Dan Hoke.

Cover design by LACreative
Page design by Win-Win Words

ISBN: 978-0-692-72307-4

Printed in the United States of America

Dedicated to my hometown

Contents

Foreword

M IKE LEACH AND I FIRST CROSSED PATHS SEVENTEEN YEARS AGO IN NOR-
MAN, OKLAHOMA, when he joined the staff of Bob Stoops at the University of Oklahoma as offensive coordinator-quarterbacks coach. I had retired from coaching, and he was one of the bright minds of innovative offense in the collegiate ranks.

It didn't take long for me to recognize the impact Mike had on OU football with his wide-open style of offense. Although he was only there for one year, he helped build the foundation that led to the Sooners' national championship in 2000.

Also, during that season, Mike and I developed a lasting friendship. We held many a conversation on football and philosophy over dinner at Othello's Italian Restaurant in Norman.

Mike is a bright guy, and I'm not just talking about his football IQ. He's just as comfortable talking about music or politics as he is about the targeting rule. And I really liked his inquisitive nature, which revealed a real appreciation for the history and traditions of college football.

His passing offense is both exciting and productive in putting points on the scoreboard. Mike has always said – and I agree – that his Air Raid attack has a lot in common with the Wishbone we ran in Norman. As he has said, both are option offenses that rely a great deal on distribution – that is, making sure all of your skill players have an opportunity to touch the ball. It's just that one offense throws the ball, while the other offense pitches the ball.

Beyond the X's and O's, I think Mike is just plain good for the game of college football. His sometimes unconventional approach adds an unpredictable flair to the game and generates interest from the fans and media alike. He says what he thinks and offers his honest opinion, not only on football, but on life in general. As a former coach, I find that refreshing. At the same time, Mike doesn't shy away from controversy, while standing up for what he believes in. Again, a most admirable trait, in my book.

After leaving OU, Mike did a tremendous job in building a consistent winner during his ten years at Texas Tech. I continue to follow the impressive progress he is making today as he rebuilds the Washington State program.

Any football fan will certainly enjoy this collection of Mike Leach quotes ... and you might even learn something along the way. In fact, it was only after reading a quote from Mike in this book that I discovered that he considered me to be a fashion expert — on jeans, at least:

"Barry Switzer understands, and this is an important point that's been lost in this metrosexual generation, there are not twenty-five types of jeans — there are two and they are either made by Levi's or Wrangler. And all that other stuff is slacks. Anybody that views anything else as jeans that extends beyond Levi's or Wrangler is simply incorrect, and Barry understands that in great detail."

This is just one of about seven hundred quotes that I think you will find to be highly entertaining.

— Barry Switzer

(In sixteen seasons as head coach at the University of Oklahoma, Barry Switzer and his ground-oriented wishbone offense set numerous records en route to three national championships — 1974, 1975, 1985. The Hall of Fame coach posted a record of 157-29-4 at OU. In 1996, he guided the Dallas Cowboys to a Super Bowl title. Switzer is one of only three coaches in history to win both a college football national championship and a Super Bowl.)

Acknowledgments

A NY AUTHOR WILL TELL YOU THAT WRITING A BOOK IS A LABORIOUS TASK. It requires a great deal of time, patience, research, writing, editing, rewriting, more time, more patience, more research, more writing, more editing, more rewriting, and well, you get the idea. Perseverance might be the word to best sum it all up.

Almost any author will also tell you that writing a book is a labor of love — for all of the blood, sweat, and tears hopefully result in some sense of satisfaction and accomplishment for both the writer and the reader.

I can truly say that I enjoyed every single moment of working on *Squib-Kick It to a Fat Guy* – even the many late nights of research and writing while wearing out the batteries on my iPod.

Squib-Kick It to a Fat Guy would not have been possible without the dedicated work of many members of the media who have chronicled the career of Mike Leach over the years. These men and women of print, internet, radio, and TV have unfailingly covered games, attended news conferences, and conducted interviews, all to give us a behind-the-scenes and insightful perspective.

Special thanks to Don Williams and the cast at the *Lubbock Avalanche-Journal* for their day-to-day coverage of the Texas Tech life and times of Mike Leach over a ten-year period. Much of their insight and comprehensive work is found in this book. Kudos in this regard also to Betsy Blaney of the Associated Press (Lubbock bureau).

Likewise, thanks go to Christian Caple and Jacob Thorpe at the *Spokane Spokesman Review* and Bud Withers and Stephanie Loh at the *Seattle Times*, whose work supplied many of the Washington State quotes. The weekly official WSU press conferences are required watching, as well as a wonderful source for Leachisms. And a special acknowledgment to Alex Ybarra, formerly of the *Daily Toreador* (Tech student newspaper), who was the first person (I think) to use Leach's famous "little girlfriend" quote while reporting on spring workouts. Also, I want to recognize Brent Schrotenboer (*Avalanche-Journal, USA Today*, etc.) for the great Leach quotes he has used in a number of well-written and entertaining feature stories.

It is impossible to thank everyone individually, but a complete list of sources is found in the back of the book.

Also deserving of a tip of the hat is Bill Stevens, associate director of athletics at Washington State, for his assistance and use of photographs from his department. I also appreciate the cooperation of Coach Leach on this project. (Note to Coach: I did my best not to misquote you within these pages.)

The foreword to the book was made possible through the cooperation of Coach Barry Switzer, Cheena Pazzo, and Sean Burrage.

Dan Hoke of Southeastern Oklahoma State University did his best in contributing the author's photo.

This book made it to the finish line in part because of the talented work of Tennessee resident Mike Towle of Win-Win Words.

I must also thank my dad, Bob Burton, and brother, Brian, for their behind-the-scenes support. Finally, I want to thank Michelle, counselor extraordinaire and former high school English teacher, for lending her tireless (and superior) editing skills from the very beginning.

Introduction

SINCE THE BEGINNING OF TIME, COACHES HAVE BORED US TO TEARS WITH their bland, politically correct public comments. This self-serving phenomenon is known simply as "Coachspeak."

Coachspeak is that universal language coaches use when talking with the media. The primary goal is to never say anything that could be interpreted as offensive to anyone, while simultaneously lavishing flattery on the opponent. A liberal dose of meaningless clichés is also common. No matter how dire the situation is or how hated the rival might be, coaches can always fall back on this time-tested dialect.

"We don't have a lot of experience or depth, but we have a chance to be competitive if we can avoid injuries," and "I have a great deal of respect for Coach Schmo and his program," are among the more common refrains uttered in Coachspeak.

And then along comes someone unique — such as Mike Leach — part ruffled, off-the-cuff John Madden, part cerebral Bud Wilkinson, part taskmaster Bill Parcells, part sardonic Abe Lemons.

As you will see, Coachspeak is pretty much nonexistent in *Squib-Kick it to a Fat Guy – and 699 More Memorable Quotes from the Playbook of Coach Mike Leach.*

Instead, allow us to introduce a new vocabulary word — "Leachspeak."

"Leachspeak," much of what is presented in this book, has evolved from the scripture of Bear Bryant, the folksy, descriptive stories of Darrell Royal and Spike Dykes, the one-line humor of Lou Holtz, the confidence of Barry Switzer, and even the head-scratching, syntax-challenged misstatements of Bill Peterson, whose coaching stops included Florida State, Rice, and the NFL's Houston Oilers.

In today's college football world, Leach stands head and shoulders above his coaching peers when it comes to quotability. Sure, Michigan's Jim Harbaugh offers up an occasional cocky quote fit for bulletin board material, and LSU's Les Miles utters truly bizarre sentences from time to time, but in terms of consistent quality, no one tops Leach.

Squib-Kick It to a Fat Guy . . .

Whether it be Aggies, referees, empty corpses, zombies, players, their fat little girlfriends or tattoos, there are no taboos when it comes to "Leachspeak." Well, except for any discussion of injuries, because, well, there are, if he has any say, no injuries on a Leach-coached team.

"Coachspeak kinda bores me a little bit, too," Leach told (Portland, Oregon) KXL radio's John Canzano. "Obviously, there's stuff as a coach that you have to be guarded on — I don't think it's necessarily secrets, but you've got to weigh the interests of 125 players and a bunch of coaches and the rest. To me, the human interest stories on players and whatnot are the most interesting, which in part is why I think it's an insult to journalism to sit and talk about the injuries all the time."

In the fall of 2009, during an off week while coaching at Texas Tech, Leach was invited to the ESPN studios in Bristol, Connecticut, for a "car wash" round of interviews. It just so happened that was the week after his Red Raiders had been upset by Texas A&M. In postgame remarks, Leach had publicly blamed his players' "fat little girlfriends" for the team's lack of focus (more on that later).

When asked by ESPN's Mike Greenberg about his philosophy of dealing with the media, Leach put it this way: "I try to be honest first," he said. "Maybe I ought to shift the priorities a little bit. I think things have gotten a little too homogenized in this country, and I think people should be allowed to speak their mind. Otherwise, we're going to bore each other to death."

On this count, Leach and businessman/2016 presidential candidate Donald Trump, the king of political incorrectness, would agree. Ironically, Leach and Trump are friends. That dates back to 2005, when the Tech coach, while in New York, called Trump's office. Trump was not available at the time, but he called the coach back a few weeks later. In 2007, Trump introduced the Red Raiders' starting lineup in a televised game with Oklahoma. And a few years later, Trump wrote a letter to the University of Miami president urging her to hire Leach.

On the subject of quotes, the late, great sportswriter Leonard Koppett believed they were overused, at least by the print media.

"Quotes, in my opinion, are the bane of today's journalism," Koppett wrote in his 2003 book, *The Rise and Fall of the Press Box*. "They make what people say more important than what people do, and rarely capture in print the true meaning and flavor of words that, when delivered, involved tone of voice, body language, unspoken assumptions, and context of situation. The tape recorder and microphone, unambiguously, get the exact words. Then these are picked up and repeated endlessly everywhere with or without relevance or completeness."

In an earlier book, *Sports Illusion, Sports Reality* (1991), Koppett wrote this, which further clarifies his thoughts:

"Quotes, like anything else, are only as good as their context. As a rule, a description of an action in quote form is marvelous for radio and television, and a waste of space in print. A printed quote acquires value when it is an intrinsically colorful expression, a startling statement, or a formal issue when wording is important."

Leach is an exception to Koppett's declaration. Granted, his TV interviews — complete with tone and expression — are classic. But many of his quotes also translate well into print, and as the following pages will show, many of his expressions would qualify as "colorful" or "startling."

But leave it to Lemons, the former University of Texas basketball coach (among other college teams) to best describe what doesn't translate well into print. It seems the colorful coach was displeased with the officiating in a 1977 game at Texas Tech. After the contest, Lemons voiced his thoughts by using an obscenity when referring to one of the referees. The quote somehow found its way into print.

After receiving a complaint, Texas Athletic Director Darrell Royal dutifully called Lemons into his office for an explanation.

"Darrell," admitted Lemons, "I guess chicken shit doesn't look very good in print."

Leach's unconventional rise in the coaching ranks has been well chronicled. A native of Susanville, California, he grew up in Wyoming. He never played college football. He earned his undergraduate degree in American Studies at Brigham Young University and a master's of sports science in sports coaching at the United States Sports Academy. In addition, he received a law degree at Pepperdine.

Before entering the legal profession, Leach decided to give coaching a shot and landed at such outposts as Cal-Poly, College of the Desert, Finland, Iowa Wesleyan, and Valdosta State. Spurning a law career, Leach finally joined the big time in 1997 as offensive coordinator at Kentucky.

Two years later, he took the same role at the University of Oklahoma under Bob Stoops. In late 1999, he was named head coach at Texas Tech University.

In ten years at the Lubbock school, Leach led the Red Raiders to unprecedented success and national recognition, compiling an 84-43 record and guiding the program to ten consecutive bowl appearances. Increased attendance resulted in the expansion of Jones SBC/AT&T Stadium. Along the way, the eccentric coach's teams produced some of the highest graduation rates in the country. And his Air Raid offense led the nation in passing more often than not.

The 2009 Tech media guide describes Leach as such: "Arguably one of the most innovative coaches in the country, Mike Leach not only has transformed Texas Tech football, but also the face of college football with an all-out aerial assault."

It ended badly in Lubbock, however. In late 2009 ESPN broadcaster and former SMU and NFL running back Craig James accused Leach of mistreating his son, Adam James, a backup receiver for the Red Raiders. Although such mistreatment was never proven, Tech dismissed the popular coach. The messy affair became a public war of words and led Leach to pursue — unsuccessfully — legal action.

Leach and his family moved to Key West, Florida, where he spent time writing a best-selling book with Bruce Feldman, in addition to traveling, lecturing, and offering radio and TV football commentary.

After staying out of coaching for two years, Leach emerged in Pullman, Washington, in 2012 as head coach of the Washington State Cougars, a member of the Pac-12 conference.

And just what is that "squib-kick it to a fat guy" quote all about?

Read on, the answer is found in this book.

Squib-Kick It to a Fat Guy . . .

1
Great Expectations

"We're really excited about having Mike as the next football coach. I think Mike, with his exciting, wide-open style of offense, will excite the fans, gain national recognition for the university, and attract top recruits. It will bring a whole new level of excitement to Texas Tech football."

> — **Gerald Myers**, Texas Tech athletic director, on the hiring of Mike Leach as head football coach, December 10, 1999

By his own admission, Texas Tech football coach Spike Dykes was feeling a little stale as the 1999 season began. In directing the Red Raiders for thirteen years, the affable, folksy, sixty-one-year-old coach had provided the stability the Tech program had so desperately needed. The five Tech coaches prior to the Dykes regime had lasted an average of three and a half seasons, each eventually leaving town for widely different reasons.

There was gruff Jim Carlen, a religious disciplinarian and recruiting whiz who enjoyed an 11-1 season and a five-year (1970-74) record of 37-20-2 before departing after clashing with university administrators. Carlen, at age thirty-seven, had been hired from West Virginia.

Next came one of the brightest young coaches in the nation: thirty-one-year-old Steve Sloan from Vanderbilt. Sloan's Red Raiders had a fabulous 10-2 season in 1976, but he exited after three seasons for supposedly greener pastures (ultimately, he never again had a winning season in nine years at Mississippi and Duke).

Rex Dockery, a thirty-six-year-old assistant under Sloan, then took the reins, enjoying limited success (15-16-2) before resigning after four years to accept the Memphis State job.

Dockery was followed by North Texas State head coach Jerry Moore, whose background included stints as an assistant at SMU and Nebraska. Moore was dismissed after five seasons (1981-85) at Tech, compiling a 16-37-2 record. Moore later earned national recognition at Appalachian State, where he won three national championships in Division I FCS/I-AA competition.

After removing Moore, Tech officials looked to Austin and found their man in longtime University of Texas assistant David McWilliams.

The forty-four-year-old coach didn't disappoint, guiding the Raiders to a 7-4 mark and a bowl berth in 1986. But just as the Tech program appeared to be on the rise, McWilliams abruptly resigned to return to UT as head coach after Fred Akers was fired. Tech fans were furious at McWilliams for what they considered a rapid breach of loyalty.

Enter Spike Dykes, an assistant on both Moore's and McWilliams's respective staffs. Dykes was named interim coach for the bowl game and afterward had the interim tag removed.

Although the Raiders lost the '86 Independence Bowl (to Ole Miss), over the next thirteen years, Dykes would achieve a record of 82-67-1, the first appearance for the school in the Cotton Bowl, and five other bowl outings.

Along the way, there were outstanding seasons (9-3 in 1989 and 1995) and not-so- outstanding seasons (4-7 in 1990 and 5-6 in 1988 and 1992).

Dykes's average season at Tech was 6-5 and his best regular season finish in a conference (Southwest or Big 12) was second place. He was a very respectable 6-7 against rivals Texas and Texas A&M, but struggled with an embarrassing 1-3 mark against lesser weights such as North Texas. His last four seasons didn't offer much optimism, as his teams went 7-5, 6-5, 7-5, and 6-5.

Dykes's final season of highs and lows was typical of his time at Tech: his last Red Raiders team defeated rivals Texas A&M and Oklahoma (the latter in come-from-behind fashion in the season finale).

Prior to that, though, Tech suffered a home loss to North Texas and blowout losses to Texas, Missouri, Oklahoma State, and Arizona State.

With grumbling from some boosters, the popular old-school coach called it a career. He did so gracefully, departing as the winningest football coach in school history.

In his 2004 book, *Tales from the Texas Tech Sideline*, Dykes wrote: "But while I was there (Tech), we went through four or five presidents and four athletic directors. Now, you know those people may have wanted somebody who was their own guy — not me — as their football coach. That's the way it is . . . I have to say it was mostly a mutual admiration society when I left, but I still imagine there were two or three people on that board of directors (regents) who were tickled to death that I decided to step down."

So who would the Red Raiders call on to reinvigorate their program and take it to the next level?

Tech officials were determined to hire someone who would bring an exciting style of play to town. In so doing, they focused on New Mexico State head coach Tony Samuel and two young up-and-coming offensive coordinators — Rich Rodriguez at Clemson and Mike Leach at the University of Oklahoma. Rodriguez was considered to be the frontrunner for the job, but he withdrew his name from consideration late in the process. Samuel had earlier made the same decision.

On December 9, 1999, thirty-eight-year-old Mike Leach was named the thirteenth head football coach at Texas Tech. As they say, the rest is history.

"One thing that's always been important to me with regard to Texas Tech — and the reason I came here — it wasn't as much about where they were at or what they were doing as their goals and objectives — where they're headed, where they want to be, and what they were going to do to try to get there. That was the biggest factor, and also support. I didn't want to be in a position where things were splintered up, where anytime you hoped to accomplish something, that there was going to be resistance on all sides. From an administrative stand-point, it's pretty united."

— **Leach**, *preparing to start his first season at Texas Tech, 2000*

"MIKE'S MARCHING ORDERS ARE TO NEVER HAVE A LOSING SEASON AND EVERY FIVE YEARS WE SHOULD WIN THE BIG 12. WE SHOULD ALWAYS BE IN THE TOP HALF OF OUR DIVISION. I THINK THOSE ARE REASONABLE EXPECTATIONS."

— *James Sowell, Texas Tech board of regents chairman, 2000*

"WE FEEL WITHOUT ANY QUESTION THAT WE HAVE FOUND THE COM-PLETE COACH AND LANDED THE BRIGHTEST RISING COACHING STAR IN COLLEGE FOOTBALL TODAY. WE'RE LOOKING FORWARD TO A LONG AND PROSPEROUS RELATIONSHIP."

— **Gerald Myers**, *Texas Tech athletic director, on Leach's hiring*

"Folks kept telling me I was supposed to have it. After this many years, you just kind of go stand in the same place and fold your arms the same way."

— **Leach**, *when asked if he had a lump in his throat in anticipation of his first game as a head coach, 2000*

"Well, outside of Lubbock, expectations aren't very high. But it's okay; we play in Lubbock a lot this season."

— Leach, on his team's expectations in 2006

"We aren't exactly America's team."

— Leach, on the low-profile, but up-and-coming Texas Tech football program

"I ASKED ATHLETIC DIRECTOR BILL MOOS TO SELECT THE BEST HEAD FOOTBALL COACH IN THE COUNTRY, AND I AM CONVINCED THAT HE HAS DONE EXACTLY THAT."

— Elson Floyd, Washington State president, on the hiring of Leach, 2011

"I HAVE SPOKEN ABOUT THE NEED TO RE-ENERGIZE OUR FAN BASE AND TAKE COUGAR FOOTBALL TO THE NEXT LEVEL. I BELIEVE THE HIRING OF MIKE LEACH ACCOMPLISHES BOTH OF THOSE GOALS."

— Bill Moos, Washington State athletic director

"It's the best administration I've ever been around. It's really a tight teamwork thing, which is unusual nowadays in college athletics, to be honest with you. Usually, there's too many people involved, too many cooks in the kitchen, too many people tugging at one another and battling each other. It's typical, not unusual. Here, there's really just a good teamwork atmosphere. Everybody pulling for the other person, very supportive."

— Leach, on Washington State

"COACH LEACH WAS SOMEONE I ENJOYED PLAYING FOR, AND IF I WAS A HIGH SCHOOL KID NOW AND I WAS BEING RECRUITED, I WOULD FEEL COMFORTABLE WITH COACH LEACH. HE EXPECTS GREATNESS. EVEN AS A REDSHIRT QUARTERBACK, WHEN I WAS THIRD OR FOURTH STRING ON SCOUT TEAM, HE EXPECTED ME TO BE GREAT IN PRACTICE. IT'S NOT JUST ON THE FOOTBALL FIELD; HE EXPECTS YOU TO BE GREAT OFF THE FIELD. YOU ARE GOING TO GO TO CLASS, YOU ARE GOING TO GRADUATE. A LOT OF GUYS WHO DIDN'T GO TO THE NEXT LEVEL (THE NFL) HAVE JOBS AND ARE SUCCESSFUL OFF THE FIELD BECAUSE OF THE EXPECTATIONS PUT ON THEM WHILE THEY WERE AT TEXAS TECH."

— *Cody Hodges, former Texas Tech quarterback*

On whether he felt any added pressure from fans while preparing for a "big" game:

"That has virtually no impact. They've already got all I've got. I do the best I can every play and every snap. If somebody sends me the e-mail (that says), 'I'm really happy about what happened,' well, that's good. I'm glad you're happy, but I'm happy, too, because I worked all week at this. If somebody's really unhappy, you might think you're unhappy, but you're not nearly as unhappy as I am. If you think you're unhappy as I am, you're kidding yourself. So they already have everything I've got. I recognize when I get to the end of the week that I've done the best I can, and your best is always enough and just leave it at that."

— *Leach*

Washington State Coach Mike Leach was named co-Pac 12 coach of the year following a 9-4 season in 2015.

"I always think we're going to beat everybody. My process goes a little like this: Early in the week, I'm not sure we can beat Lubbock High School. By the end of the week, I'm convinced we can beat the New England Patriots. As far as putting our best foot forward, expectations are a big part of it. With that said, the 2010 group, which I didn't get to coach — that was going to be our best team. We had everybody back from 2009, when we won nine games."

— *Leach*

"A lot of winning is expecting to win, not just before the game, but at various points when things get tough, various points when there are opportunities to capitalize on something, to go out there and take it."

— *Leach*

"Hopefully, as you mention, our pattern continues. I didn't realize that we were in this abyss of positive karma that may help lead us in that direction. That's good. Hold that thought."

— *Leach, when told that Texas Tech had accomplished most everything other than play in the Bowl Championship Series*

"People are capable of a lot more than they think they're capable of."

— *Leach*

"That whole mentality that it's not important to improve, just as long as everybody gets a ribbon for participating, that's one of the biggest things you have to change when you come to a program. I'm not prepared to say we've done it across the board, but we're certainly working in that direction."

— *Leach, at Washington State*

"For too long around this university, expectations to perform and all that's been too low. Unless we as coaches, we as players change that . . . it's not going to get changed from the outside. I mean everybody's going to have twenty pats on their back before they get back to their house. We got to change that. We've got to expect more of ourselves, and we've got to get more out of ourselves, starting with the coaches."

— *Leach, after Washington State's disappointing opening-season loss to Rutgers in 2014*

"Overcoming adversity is a big item in my life. The idea of achieving and overcoming something difficult is something I really admire. Everybody wants a challenge, especially coaches. It's the most volatile profession outside of acting."

— Leach

"It doesn't have to be that way; it's just how it transpired. I kind of hate to admit this. It's kind of like a term paper. You put it off."

— Leach, on his late night work habits

"Oklahoma State is now the biggest game in the history of this year."

— Leach, after Texas Tech upset top-ranked Texas, looking ahead to the next game, 2008

"People ask me, 'Why Washington State?' And once I get past in the back of my mind thinking, 'Well, that's a stupid question' (audience cheers) and then ... I roll that through my mind and I don't say it. And then I immediately blurt out the obvious answer ... the commitment to excellence in every phase of the university, the excitement around the community, and the fact that you can win here and win big, I believe."

— Leach, when introduced as the new Washington State coach, 2012

"MIKE LEACH HAS DONE A FABULOUS JOB IN HIS SHORT TIME AT WASHINGTON STATE. EXTENDING HIS CONTRACT THROUGH THE 2018 SEASON WILL ENSURE A BRIGHT FUTURE FOR COUGAR FOOTBALL. HE HAS ELEVATED THE PROGRAM ON THE FIELD, IN THE COMMUNITY, AND IN THE CLASSROOM. I BELIEVE HE IS AMONG THE BEST COLLEGE FOOTBALL COACHES IN AMERICA AND IS A FANTASTIC FIT IN PULLMAN."

— Bill Moos, Washington State athletic director, November 2013

2
Philosophically Speaking

"Timeouts are a little bit like money. You don't want to die with them and give them to your kids. So you might as well use them if you need them."

— **Leach**, providing TV analysis on the
North Carolina State-Central Florida game, 2010

When it comes to philosophy and coaching strategy, Mike Leach has his own unique ideas. Like disdaining a punt and going for it on fourth down no matter what the field position and game situation might be.

Perhaps no other coach in the history of football utilizes timeouts quite like Leach does. Most coaches save timeouts for clock management purposes at the end of a half or game. Not Leach. He never hesitates to use one, if not all, of his timeouts early in the first and/or second half.

Many times, Leach will call an early timeout to slow down the momentum of the opposition. If their offense is moving the ball to begin the second half or during another critical juncture of the game, Leach will call timeout to alter the tempo, much like a basketball coach, while offering his team a stern lecture on the sidelines.

He figures his high-powered Air Raid offense can score quickly when needed, so why save all those timeouts?

"I told him to fix his helmet, which I thought was a pretty good coaching point at the time."

> — *Leach, on what he told a quarterback whose helmet repeatedly fell off*

"The plan was to squib-kick it to a fat guy. Of course, the fat guys at Texas are nimble, and they have good hands."

> — *Leach, after two penalties had Texas Tech kicking off from its own eight-yard line with one second to play and holding a one-point lead, 2008*

"Yeah, I say, 'Go down there and score.'"

> — *Leach, when asked if he gave his team any special advice for scoring on the first possession of a game*

"You know, it's not as hard as you think. (You tell him), 'Hey, raise your elbow up.'"

> — *Leach, to reporters, on advising Texas Tech quarterback Taylor Potts on how to change his sidearm release to a more conventional release*

"I wasn't happy with that punt at all. That's why they don't let coaches go armed on the sideline for that very reason. And I'm not sure having those Texas Rangers nearby is a good idea either."

> — *Leach, on a fumbled punt*

"We had quite a ways to go to get a first down. It was kind of a no-brainer, really. I guess it's a little like when Babe Ruth strikes out three times in a row. It makes it more likely he'll hit it the next time."

> — *Leach, on not hesitating to send in Alex Trlica to attempt a game-winning, forty-nine-yard field goal in overtime against UTEP. Trlica, who had missed two kicks in the fourth quarter, made this one, and Texas Tech won, 38-35.*

"One of the few things that doesn't change is the dimension of the field and the football. There's no difference between doing it in junior high and high school and college and the NFL. It kind of remains the same. There's a ball, there's air, there's a foot, and you kick it."

> — *Leach, breaking down the dynamics of the placekicker position*

On the importance of tempo for players:
"When they fail, they become frustrated. When they have success, they want to become the thinking-man's football team. They start having these quilting bees, these little bridge parties at the line of scrimmage."

> — *Leach believes the team that wins is the team that moves fastest; he also believes both failure and success slow players down.*

"You're in the presence of a guy that manages to be a part of 681 yards of total offense but only produces twenty-one points. You won't see that for the rest of your lives."

> — *Leach, after Texas Tech's 49-21 loss to North Carolina State, 2003*

"I was hoping we'd whack him before he was able to throw it. Then I was hoping we'd intercept it. Then I was satisfied with the fact that we batted it away."

> — *Leach, on Oklahoma State quarterback Bobby Reid's pass falling incomplete in the end zone as time expired, preserving a 30-24 victory for Texas Tech, 2006*

"We talked at halftime that we had a great opportunity to make history, and the reason people come to Texas Tech is to play all sixty minutes."

> — *Leach, after a record come-from-behind victory over Minnesota in the 2006 Insight Bowl. After falling behind 38-7 with 7:47 remaining in the third quarter, Texas Tech rallied to score thirty-one unanswered points to send the game to overtime. The Gophers kicked a field goal in overtime, but the Red Raiders responded with a touchdown to win, 44-41.*

"I hoped so. I'd like to think so, because the thing is, on a deal like that, it only takes a handful of doubters to contaminate the entire group. It's not like you can weather a whole lot of doubters. I think it's important, coaches and players combined, to not have any doubters in a situation like that, to give yourself the best chance to be successful."

> — *Leach, when asked if his players believed him the time he told them at halftime of a game in which they trailed Minnoesota, 35-7, that they could rally and win. They did both.*

"WE WERE DOWN, 21-0. LEACH CALLED US UP AND (CURSED AT) US ABOUT A HUNDRED TIMES, AND WE TURNED IT AROUND AND PLAYED WELL. WE WERE ALREADY IN THE DOGHOUSE WITH HIM (AFTER A LOSS THE PREVIOUS WEEK TO NEW MEXICO) AND THEN WE GOT DOWN TO THEM (TCU). THAT GROUP, WE WERE PRETTY FEISTY GUYS, A BUNCH OF OVERACHIEVERS, SO WE WORKED HARD."

— *Mike Smith, Texas Tech interim defensive coordinator, who played linebacker for Tech in a 2004 comeback win over TCU*

"Cal was playing harder than we were, so we sort of had a get-in-touch-with-your-feelings kind of conversation where everybody got kind, fuzzy-goosey feelings for each other, and our intensity increased."

— *Leach, on his team's turnaround after trailing, 14-7, and when he called a timeout and brought the squad together for an intense lecture. Tech rallied to win the 2004 Holiday Bowl, 45-31.*

"I'm here for sixty minutes, no matter what. Everyone here is figuring on staying for the entire game. We've got nowhere else to go."

— *Leach, on the importance of playing a full sixty minutes, after Texas Tech's 31-30 comeback win over Kansas in 2004. The Red Raiders overcame a twenty-five-point deficit.*

"We just weren't doing what we could do. All we have to do is do our jobs just like we did the first half, and part of you doing your job is attacking the other guy. Sometimes there's this mentality which makes me vomit — we're ahead by ten or seventeen with most of the second half to play. Let's preserve the win. Somebody catches the ball short and he goes into the fetal position like he got shot. This smart-player crap, which drives me crazy."

— *Leach, on what he said to his team during a third-quarter lull*

"At some point, we have to stop being in the position to have to make amazing comebacks."

— *Leach, after Texas Tech rallied from an eighteen-point deficit to beat Texas A&M in overtime, 48-47, 2002*

"I think we were overly fired up — we wanted to be good too badly. It's like I said in the locker room, we took our bodies out there, but we didn't take our heads. We went out there, tried too hard, pressed and it blew up all over us. There was no method to our madness."

— *Leach, after Texas Tech was thrashed by Nebraska, 56-3*

"The thing is, when you play somebody that good, you've got to play in control. We did against Texas. We did against Oklahoma State. We didn't against Oklahoma, and I regret that. I'm going to search why we were too geeked up. We were out there with our hair on fire more than we were executing."

— *Leach, on previously undefeated Texas Tech's 65-21 loss to Oklahoma, 2008*

"Defensively, they like to hide the peanuts under the jar, change up the fronts, and bring people from different spots."

— *Leach, on playing the University of New Mexico and its variety of blitzes, 2000*

"We've got plenty to be concerned about without really worrying about that. But that's on our top one hundred list of things to talk about and make sure we address."

— *Leach, when asked about his Texas Tech team trying to end TCU's twelve-game winning streak*

"These guys were a bowl team last year, they had a real good season last year, and the other thing is these guys are already talking about running the score up on us. So if we are lucky, maybe we can keep it close."

— Leach, on not looking past UTEP, 2001
(The game was cancelled because of the 9/11 tragedy.)

"Shortly after they invented fire, they invented the notion that you keep the ball as long as you possibly can and try to keep explosive offenses off the field. But usually that breaks down, because if they fail on a drive or something, and you succeed on yours, you're going to come out on top."

— Leach, on the use of a ball-control offense
to counter a team with an explosive offense

"A lot of times the media thinks football's a series of tricks. What happened to Vince Lombardi and execution and all that? It's execution more than it's a series of tricks."

— Leach

"They used to always talk about some secret recipe. Kentucky Fried Chicken, Colonel Sanders, he had this recipe for finger food. I drove by it one time at Kentucky; I wanted to know where the vault for the recipe was. Contrary to belief, we don't have a vault."

— Leach, on his "simple" Air Raid offense

"We go into a game with probably sixty-five plays, and they may be the same play, different formation, or something like that. But after working at it all week, we're expecting some of them to work, and those ones that work, we'd like to call them again. That, and the fact that in the organized confusion and chaos that is a football sideline, I can't fit through that many (plays). I've always wondered how you broadcasters worked through all the paper and stuff like that. I would guess that you were the kids in high school that were really good at term papers and things like that."

> — *Leach, on his offensive game plan*

"If we'd thrown it 110 times, we would have won. I mean, it's pretty indisputable if we get that many plays, then we're probably going to win. So, no, the more plays you get, the better off you are."

> — *Leach, reflecting on the 2013 Washington State-Oregon game, in which the Cougars threw eighty-nine passes in a loss*

"You know, I knew we'd get at least sixty plays, so I thought there was a chance we'd throw sixty times. That's what we do. This is going to leave us with a lot of good memories the rest of our lives."

> — *Leach, after Texas Tech completed 39 of 60 passes for 520 yards and three touchdowns in a 45-31 upset of fourth-ranked California in the 2004 Holiday Bowl*

"There's a couple of ways to do it. You can wear a nice sweater and have your hands in your pocket and just shake hands with everybody and cheerlead, which has never been my way. The other way is, you contribute through your expertise. I always talk to them after each practice. Being out there elbow to elbow calling plays, you'll see everybody out there on the practice field. Anybody on defense that does anything pretty good, I'll be there front and center every day, up close in the middle of the action."

> *— **Leach**, when asked how an offense-minded coach like himself demonstrates to his defense that he is also their coach*

"I think what we're going do is split the team in half and let them play. I don't want any of those scoring systems that require an accountant to sort it out. I hate that. Well, you're out there trying to run plays and you're standing there on the sideline and every-one's murmuring and wondering, 'Well, do we get one point . . .' I hate that."

> *— **Leach**, on the format of a spring game. Some coaches use a complicated formula for scoring, with the defense getting points for stops, etc.*

"Watch the practices from start to finish if you like. Bring your family, bring your friends, bring a sack lunch if you want to."

> *— **Leach**, on his open practices at Texas Tech his first year*

"The interesting thing about football is that football is the only sport where you quit playing when you get a lead. In golf, you keep trying to score well when you're ahead. In basketball, they don't quit shooting when they're ahead. In hockey, they don't quit shooting when they're ahead. In boxing, you don't quit punching when you're ahead. But in football, somehow, magically, you're supposed to quit playing when you're ahead. Well, I don't subscribe to that. I don't do it like that. And, you know, the truth of the matter is, Nebraska never has either."

— *Leach*, *after Texas Tech beat Nebraska, 70-10, in 2004*

"I remember my first year in Nebraska, they slaughtered us, like 1,000-3 (56-3). They tried to score every time they touched the ball."

— *Leach*, *responding to criticism that instead of taking a knee, he had his team continue to throw passes into the end zone as the clock ran out in a 27-13 Texas Tech win over SMU, 2004*

"It's not possible for Nebraska as an institution to criticize anybody for a big score."

— *Leach*, *after Texas Tech walloped Nebraska, 70-10. During its earlier glory days as a perennial national power, Nebraska frequently posted lopsided victories.*

"I'VE GOT NO PROBLEM WITH (THE CHALLENGE). IF THE DAY EVER COMES, WE'RE GOING TO TRY TO HANG SEVENTY-FIVE (POINTS) ON THEIR ASS. I GUARANTEE YOU THAT."

— *Guy Morriss*, *Baylor coach, after Leach successfully challenged a fumble recovery call late in Texas Tech's 55-21 victory*

"I think under the best circumstances, football's frustrating. All teams want to do well. All teams want to play well. I would just hope we would be lucky enough to score seventy-six, you know?"

> *— **Leach**, when told that Baylor coach Guy Morriss said his team would score seventy-five points on Texas Tech if given the opportunity.*

"I don't get offended by very much."

> *— **Leach***

"If there is a controversy, it really is a stupid controversy. Anywhere there's a controversy on that, that's a starvation for controversy. This country, in general, is a master at finding offense to almost anything."

> *— **Leach**, on Baylor's being upset at him for challenging an official's call with Texas Tech leading by thirty-four points late in the game*

"I've spent a lot of time coaching our players to play hard, finish, score, all that stuff, and we don't change gears on that. I told them before the game: Your performance will be judged by your doing your best and making routine plays. When I stop the projector, I'm not going to look at the down, I'm not going to look at the distance, and I'm not going to look at the time left. If I'm going to preach that, that's what I want to get out of them. You only get so many plays; you better make the most of them."

> *— **Leach**, on continuing to throw the football near the end of a 27-13 win over SMU*

"THAT'S TOTAL BULLSHIT THAT HE THREW THE BALL AT THE END OF THE GAME LIKE HE DID. AND YOU CAN PRINT THAT AND YOU CAN SEND IT TO HIM, AND HE CAN COMMENT, TOO. I THINK IT'S LOW CLASS AND IT'S BULLSHIT TO THROW THE BALL WHEN THE GAME IS COMPLETELY OVER AGAINST OUR KIDS THAT ARE BASICALLY OUR SCOUT TEAM."

— Nick Alliotti, Oregon defensive coordinator, after Leach kept his starters in during the fourth quarter of a game in which Washington State trailed 62-24 at the time. Alliotti later apologized for his postgame comments.

"I don't criticize other teams or coaches. I focus on coaching my team."

— Leach, when asked about Alliotti's comments

"You never have, nor will you ever hear me make personnel suggestions to the other team, because it's none of my business."

— Leach, responding to New Mexico coach Rocky Long's comment that the Texas Tech coach left his starters in late in the game to pad their stats

"I've never held it against somebody that they scored a bunch of points against us. I've never taken responsibility for scoring a bunch of points on somebody else either. As a coach, your job isn't to worry about the other team. Your job is to worry about making your team the best it can be, and if you don't like what the other guy's doing, stop it or change it, because that's what your job is."

— Leach

"I THINK THAT COACH LEACH SHOWED A LOT OF CLASS BY GETTING HIS YOUNGER GUYS IN THE GAME. THEY MAY NEED THOSE GUYS DOWN THE STRETCH THIS SEASON, AND IT IS GOOD EXPERIENCE FOR THEM. I THOUGHT AS A TEAM THEY SHOWED A LOT OF CLASS, AND THAT IS SOMETHING I WILL NOT FORGET."

*— **Lou West**, Indiana State coach, after a 63-7 loss to Texas Tech. Tech led 58-0 early in the third quarter.*

"I could care less. What do I care? If we don't like it, stop it. Who cares? You think there's some level of satisfaction if I deduct one point from however many it was they beat us by, and our pitiful effort, and our refusal to line up to it? If we're too stupid to line up to it, it's our own damn fault."

*— **Leach**, on Utah's attempting a two-point conversion with a 37-0 lead against Washington State*

"I've been in this boat before as far as you win, but you're kind of disappointed how you did it. It's kind of like doing surgery with a chainsaw instead of a scalpel. We had pieces and parts flying everywhere. It turned out in our favor. We've just got to clean it up the next time around."

*— **Leach**, disappointed in his team's play, even after a 24-3 Texas Tech win over New Mexico*

"We just need to polish things up. Football is a constant state of corrections. We just have some screwdriver-type stuff, nothing major."

*— **Leach**, on preparing his Texas Tech team to play New Mexico*

"He's suspended until we get to the bottom of it and then figure out the details. I don't want any distractions. If there's distractions and you're trying to practice, remove distractions, and practice so you can do it with a better direction and more clearly. Anytime somebody gets arrested, it's disappointing, but you move on. We just need to focus on football. So as far as his deal, that's really all I have to say. We've got people out here that made a bunch of plays, and so those guys count more than ones that get arrested."

— Leach, on suspending a player who had been arrested

"We've got 130 people (players on the roster) out there. I'm getting sick and tired of wasting time on a handful of people who can't do what they're told. It's like the 95-5 (idea): You spend 95 percent of your time on 5 percent of your players. Baloney. I'm not doing that."

— Leach, on dealing with a player with recurring academic issues

"I think it'll help our team. There is a certain addition by subtraction that exists in football. Guys that are willing to pull the right direction as a unit are more important than individuals that can strum up some flashes here and there, so I think it makes us a stronger team."

— Leach, on the fact that a Texas Tech
linebacker would not be returning for his senior season

"I've given up on following that saga. If he's here, I'll coach him, and if he's not, I won't. There's a lot of twists and turns, and we've been hearing that something's going to surface the next day, and so it goes."

— Leach, awaiting an academic appeal from the
NCAA regarding the eligibility of a Texas Tech receiver

"I think he quit. I don't know for sure. If he's going to quit, he needs to quit. I'm tired of (hearing) rumblings. Football's a deal where a guy has to very badly want to play in order to be effective. He's going to have to make those decisions himself. We're not in the business of begging guys to play."

— *Leach, when asked about a rumor that a Texas Tech offensive lineman had quit during the offseason*

"Contrary to popular belief, no train stops for Brandon Sesay."

— *Leach, on why the Texas Tech defensive end was not included on the team's pre-season roster. Sesay was dealing with eligibility issues at the time.*

"I just try to focus on what is important now and expedite things. I think that in the world of football, a lot of times there's a temptation to pick up rat droppings when elephant droppings are flying everywhere. So we try to focus on elephant droppings around here."

— *Leach*

"I think focus is something people practice and they get better at. Just like you guys (media) growing up; in my case it was the multiplication tables. I thought I'd focused all I could and then second time through I didn't get it right. Of course, my dad was pretty upset about that and decided we were going to stay up until about one o'clock that night until I got it right. Well, I learned to focus. Hey, want to go to bed, you've got to learn to focus. And, in fairness, I've never forgotten my multiplication tables, and I don't even like math."

— *Leach, on focus*

"I think this is the kind of win you can think about for about fifteen hours and then you can forget about it till your grandchildren (ask), and focus a whole lot on Oregon State."

*— **Leach**, after Washington State upset Oregon, 2015*

"I couldn't give one earthly ounce of attention to any of that. On the list of priorities, including what my next snack is going to be, that would rank way, way, way down the list. It's not a real priority. If they do a good job focusing on the next play, some of them will be lucky enough to be invited to things like that. If they don't do a very good job of focusing on the next play, they won't be. It's as simple as that."

*— **Leach**, when asked if any of his Washington State players had received post-season all-star invitations or NFL interest*

"They overplayed their coverage, he (Graham Harrell) threw it underneath and (Michael) Crabtree did a good job of turning and going straight up the field. He could have gotten out of bounds if he needed to, but he had the end zone and he got it. I think the timing of it is probably the biggest thing. There are other plays that exist like that, but the timing of it, I think, is what makes it memorable. I am glad it is on TV all the time and everybody should take close notice and write a lot of stories about it and just reflect on it fondly for decades to come."

*— **Leach**, on the game-winning pass from Graham Harrell to Michael Crabtree against Texas in 2008 and its frequent showings on highlight programs*

"It helps if you block. Like in seventh grade, the first thing, they put all of your stuff on. Your stuff's hanging all over, and they say this is how you block. What we may have to do is walk some folks, maybe all of us should go — coaches and players — down to Lubbock Junior High and work on blocking. I guess this afternoon we'll have a discussion on who's entitled to not block if they don't feel like it and who is."

— *Leach, after a poor effort by the offensive line against the University of North Texas, 2000*

"If you catch it well in junior high, through however many years — I mean it's just a ball flying through the air — there ain't nothing to that. We dropped more balls today than we did the entire week in practice. There ain't nothing wrong with our hands, legs, ears, eyes, none of that. We just got to unclutter what's in our head."

— *Leach*

"If you hit a couple guys in the face with the football, you think they'd catch it. Here's the thing about catching the football that's always amazed me. It really doesn't matter how the football's propelled. Whether it be by a fifth-grader or an all-pro quarterback or a machine. The ball is propelled and there's a ball in the air and either you catch it or you don't. We typically do in practice and then, all the sudden, our fragile little receivers get in the end zone and they get frightened, so then, all the sudden, they can't catch the ball. That's crazy. They just need to learn to be tougher. Fortunately for them, you didn't ask me if our receivers are tough or not. If you had, it wouldn't have been the answer they'd like to hear."

— *Leach, on his receivers at Washington State, 2013*

"We had a bunch of receivers just eat, ride, and warm up this last week, and they need to take it upon themselves to improve. This business that I'm going to pretend it's otherwise, that's just not the case. So I'll address that with them — and have, and will do it repeatedly."

— Leach

"They were drops. They hit guys right in the chest, hands, and gut. If they were bullets, they would have killed them."

— Leach, on his Washington State receivers and their high number of dropped passes against Southern Cal, 2014

"I think some of them need to go both ways and play on offense because they're damn sure catching it better than some of the guys on offense are. Five of the best catches of the game were all on defense."

— Leach, on the Texas Tech defense intercepting five passes, while the receivers had several drops against SMU, 2008

"The reason that they have football is to watch big people beat up on other big people. Kind of the whole physical human monster truck thing. And then after you watch that for a little bit you say, 'OK, let's see, that guy was pretty darn big. What would it look like for him to mash that little guy?'"

— Leach

"If you're going to be an offensive lineman, and you're the toughest unit on the team, then you've got to be the toughest. Go out there and whip the guy across from you just because you're tougher than he is. If that's not your mentality, you probably ought to play something else. Like Scrabble, maybe, or something like that."

— Leach

"Touchdowns are better than field goals. Saves you a lot of aggravation. I'm not a guy who really plays for field goals anyway. I hate those things."

— Leach

"Well, clearly it's mental. Guys that let stuff run around in their head. 'Oh, my gosh, I'm in college. Oh, my gosh, these guys are bigger. Oh, my gosh, they're better. Where do I get a haircut? What's the best hamburger place here? Oh, I've got English class, well Mom's not making me go, so how do I get there? Oh, this girl in English is really hot, but I'm sure she hates me.' It just goes on, and on, and on. But those that are able to seal it out, like (Washington State receiver) River Cracraft evidently, have a chance to go out there and do it like they could in high school and build on that. That's what's key. But there are some great, great players out there who go through the long windup and adjustment."

— Leach, on players adjusting from high school to college

"Whoever was your junior high coach, provided he was above average, virtually everything he told you, we're going to emphasize big time — and we're going to do that over and over. I know it sounds strange. But there's nobody so good that he doesn't need to play with low pads. There's nobody so good that they don't need to come out of their cuts quickly. There's nobody that doesn't need to be in a great stance. There's nobody that doesn't need to tackle well and block well."

— Leach, on beginning practice at Washington State, 2013

"It's always important to steadily improve your skills. That's why you practice, that's why you do the whole thing. It's always been interesting to me and I get questions like this every year. And I will every other week for the rest of the season. It will be something to the effect of, 'Well, you're playing this team and they're really good, so are you guys gonna practice extra hard this week?' Well, if we're doing our job, how can we practice extra hard? If we're out there playing as hard as we can every day, there isn't no 'extra hard' — we're already as hard as we can be. Then there's the notion that, you know this, ah, you know that practice is just a Jaycee softball league or something like that, you know, 'yuk yuk, ha ha,' oh, now that we've got somebody that's tough, let's practice hard. No, it's a series of steady improvement."

*— **Leach***

"I don't know where this stuff came about, this stick-it-over-the-goal line business, but it's dangerous. It's sloppy workmanship. There's these little fads that go on in football, stuff that's sloppy, that's bad fundamentally. It's all part of that following-the-crowd crap that I hate."

*— **Leach**, upset that Texas Tech receiver Joel Filani fumbled on the 1-yard line against Texas A&M, 2006*

"I thought we were lethargic. Today, we dealt with a bunch of people that just punched the time clock — punched in and punched out, and that was about it. It'll change, or we'll roll enough heads to make it change."

*— **Leach**, upset with a pre-season practice*

In his first fourteen seasons as a college head coach, Mike Leach has compiled a record of 105-72. His record in bowl games is 6-5.

"Our (starters) did not look good. I didn't think our first defense did, and I didn't think our first offense did. So we're going to scrimmage on Monday. Hell, if I have to keep them an extra hour, it doesn't bother me. I'm going to be alive for twenty-four hours (Monday). If they have to spend it all with me, it's just as well. I've got to spend it with somebody."

— *Leach, dissatisfied with a Texas Tech spring scrimmage*

"I watch less football than people think I do. I watch games and practice film during the day, so I don't really watch games from start to finish. My wife watches enough for all of us."

— *Leach*

"We need to be tougher in the fourth quarter. It's about as simple as that. I thought we played hard and did some good things and then our technique breaks down. I think we tell ourselves we're fatigued long before we're ever even actually fatigued. Part of being fatigued is a decision and everybody goes out here and everybody's tired. Big deal. Like the other guys on the other side aren't tired? We're jumping on the fatigue bandwagon way too quick. We need to be tougher."

— Leach, after Washington State's narrow victory over UNLV, 2012

"Well, they're just going to have to cowboy up a little bit and play fifty-seven plays. You know, God forbid a football player should have to go out and play fifty-seven plays at the ripe old age of eighteen to twenty-two. . . . I don't want to hear anything about being tired."

— Leach, after some Tech players said the Red Raiders might have been tired after North Dakota ran fifty-seven plays in a Tech victory

"When something negative happens, we can't have these basset-hound looks on the sidelines. Right now, we're too fragile. It's too easy for us to get disappointed."

— Leach, on his first Washington State squad

"We've got to get meaner. I mean, we're a team of gentlemen. There's a nastiness to this game."

— Leach

31

"I'm one of those guys that, football-wise, I'm thinking about it all the time. I might ask the janitor or whoever's just in the hall. They might throw something out like, 'Your linemen are playing real high.' All of a sudden, I'll get conscious of it. Once in a while, they're right. Once in a while, it drags my attention to something that needs to be addressed. As a coach, you're always too close to it and may not see everything. You get some nonsense, there's no question. But the nonsense, you have to sift through it quickly. Once in a while, a fresh set of eyes will see something where, in the back of my mind, I'm going, 'I'm sitting here watching it every day. How did I not see that?'"

— Leach

"It doesn't matter what you do, be it the butcher, the baker, or the candlestick maker. Be excited about what you do."

— Leach, on his philosophy

"We might say, 'If we win it, we'll be bowl-eligible,' but it's all going to be focused on Oklahoma State. All we care about is winning the next game. We're very shallow people. We don't think of the big picture ever at all, and we don't look at long-term impact on short-term deals. We don't care about any of that stuff."

— Leach, when asked about emphasizing to his team that a Texas Tech victory over Oklahoma State would make the Red Raiders bowl-eligible, 2002

"We're ahead from the standpoint that everybody knows where to line up. We're not just teaching drills. We're able to run drills and execute and build on it. So we're ahead and we're still young, but our young guys are a year older, most of them."

— Leach, on being ahead of schedule from the previous year

"You are either coaching it or you are allowing it to happen."

— *Leach*

"One thing that I've never liked is this notion of, 'Well, I coached really well, but they didn't play good.' Baloney. They didn't play because you didn't coach very good. Or 'They played great and we did a horrible job,' because I don't believe that either. Players and coaches go hand in hand. And the more that's reinforced, and the more the unit believes that, the better they're going to work together."

— *Leach*

"I just go to work every day, spend hours in the film room, go to practice, go home, and then do it all again the next day. I know I can be boring and I sound like a walking cliché, but I really do just try to get our team ready to win a game on Saturday. That's pretty much my life."

— *Leach*

"I'm not into hocus-pocus, but there's something to this."

— *Leach, on the* New Age *movement*

"I'm not a big picture guy. I live in the moment."

— *Leach*

"I'm not a big milestone guy. It's not like I'm gonna sit in a rocking chair, sip herb tea, and ask, 'What's the meaning of life.'"

— *Leach*

3
Holiday Inns,
Waffle Houses,
and Chicken Expresses

"Most coaches like Marriotts because they're nicer and closer to the airport. But I like Holiday Inns. They're convenient; they're clean; nobody messes with your bags or your car. You can just pull in and pull out."

— Leach

Prior to Leach's arrival in Pullman, Washington as head coach of the Washington State Cougars, you would have needed a compass and Rand McNally map to track the whereabouts of Mike Leach.

He was born in Susanville, California, but, by the time Leach was twelve, his family had moved to seven different locations due to his father's job as a forester: Fall River Mills, California; Alexandria, Virginia; Saratoga, Wyoming; Fort Collins, Colorado; Golden, Colorado; Sheridan, Wyoming; and, finally, Cody, Wyoming, which he considers to be his hometown. Leach's educational pursuits then took him to Provo, Utah (Brigham Young University); Malibu, California (Pepperdine University School of Law); and Daphne, Alabama (United States Sports Academy).

After that, Leach's nomadic coaching life included stops at such diverse addresses as San Luis Obispo, California (Cal Poly); Palm Desert, California (College of the Desert); Pori, Finland (Pori Bears of the European Federation of American Football); Mount Pleasant, Iowa (Iowa Wesleyan); Valdosta, Georgia (Valdosta State); Lexington, Kentucky (University of Kentucky); Norman, Oklahoma (University of Oklahoma); and Lubbock, Texas (Texas Tech). He then landed in Key West, Florida (two years out of coaching).

⤳

34

"You always stay at the same hotel because there is only one in Manhattan, Kansas. Every time we have ever been there, there is this gigantic frat party going on right next to where our meeting rooms are. They'd always stick you by that room, and there would be a bunch of drunk sororities and fraternities in there having a big time."

— Leach, on playing at Kansas State

"No matter where you are, or what time of the day or night you go there, you can always find sweet ice tea and a jukebox at a Waffle House."

— Leach, on why he considered the
Waffle House the world's best restaurant, 1997

"There's a gas station here. I don't know if you all are familiar with Lubbock. It's called Chicken Express. It's awesome if you get out this way. First off, it's just at this gas station deal. Then you know that they got that beer batter chicken stuff that it's not really fried. But, anyway, it's kind of a breaded stuff. It's great. I'm going to get me a couple."

— Leach, to reporters on a Big 12 teleconference, 2001

"These (baseball) fields in Lubbock are some of the best in the nation. And they all have these cinder block buildings, where you can take them for their stuff after the game and never leave the park. It's all kind of one-stop shopping."

— Leach, when asked if he took his son to
Sonic or Dairy Queen after Little League games

"The people are incredibly similar. They're very friendly people here. The weather is nicer here. The mountains are shorter here."

— *Leach, comparing Lubbock, Texas, to his childhood home in Wyoming*

"COACH LEACH IS THE EPITOME OF TEXAS TECH. SOMEBODY ONCE CALLED US THE ULTIMATE REBEL SCHOOL, AND THAT'S WHAT WE'RE ALL ABOUT. WE NEVER LET UP, AND WE DO WHATEVER WE WANT TO DO, AND LEACH IS A PERFECT EXAMPLE OF THAT."

— *David McDaniel, Texas Tech student, 2008*

"The one where I'm at is pretty darned good, so I'm really excited to be where I am. . . . I'm real happy at Texas Tech, and it's really a thrill to be there. I imagine the temperature (in Lubbock) is about like here (in Kansas City), but no humidity. So if you come up there, I'll show you a great steak place, and pretty soon you'll move to Lubbock, Texas. You'll have to keep that to yourself; otherwise, everybody will be there, and you and I will both want to move."

— *Leach, at the Big 12 Media Days in Kansas City, when asked by a Lubbock writer if he had a dream job somewhere, 2006*

"I THINK HE RELISHES THE ATMOSPHERE AND HISTORY OF WEST TEXAS. IT'S PERFECT FOR HIM, AS FUNNY AS IT SOUNDS."

— *Kliff Kingsbury, former Texas Tech quarterback, on Leach, 2008*

"I'll be honest with you, I'm not that particular. I'm a little bit like Apache Indians were with horses. Horses were transportation. In some tribes, horses were pets. Apaches, they were transportation. I view cars that way. I drive whatever they give me . . . with having kids and whatnot, I need a little more space than a pick-up provides. And I'm not into SUVs. Because I think SUVs are pomp and circumstance. A lot of times they're just Luminas raised off the ground. My favorite is Cadillac DeVille. In Lubbock, they gave me the fancy Cadillac, the sports car, the one that goes 160 miles per hour. Now, when am I going 160 miles per hour?"

— *Leach, on the corporate car of his choice*

"What's up with all the computer stuff on cars these days? I like my cars to be simple. If you can't put a toggle switch on it, I really don't need it. They always try to give me a big fancy rental car . . . just give me a Taurus. . . . They don't make those anymore."

— *Leach*

"I don't get motion sickness. I love reading in cars. Well, not while I'm driving so much. I try not to drive. I let others drive. . . . I read."

— *Leach*

"The tempo was really good, and the execution was sharp. I thought we were a lot more crisp than Tuesday. Some of that is due to the fact that we have another day in, and some of it is because we weren't having to wipe hail from our eyes and the footballs were playing at an official size and weight."

— *Leach, referring to the second day of spring drills at Texas Tech, after the first day of spring practice in hail and a thunderstorm made footing treacherous and footballs heavy and slippery*

"It's warmer here this week than it's going to be in Auburn. The week before, it was pretty much dead even. And the week before that, it was significantly hotter here in Pullman. And if I wasn't on my phone, I could look at my temperature thing and tell you with some detail within the accuracy that that provides."

— *Leach, on the temperatures in Pullman, Washington, 2013*

"There would be gnats all over just biting the hell out of your face, and they just — it doesn't even bother them. You're going like even down in Valdosta, because the gnats rarely got too hot, I guess. And then finally this one high school coach, as I'm recruiting there, he says, 'Try this.' Now I have big old fat lips, so it didn't work very good. But he could fire up a little puck, kind of blow the gnats off, then they had Skin So Soft, which is big, and I don't know what that is, but evidently gnats don't like it. They rub that all over. But it looked kind of oily, you know? What I think is the gnats don't care about it, but it probably puts a little sheet of oil on there so it's harder to bite you. You don't feel the bite. That's just one guy's theory. I'm sure I'm wrong."

— *Leach, on the gnats in Macon, Georgia*

"Overall, we have great weather here in Lubbock, Texas, and if you don't believe me, look at the other 80 percent of the country and you'll see what I'm talking about."

— *Leach, as a guest weather forecaster on Lubbock TV, 2005*

"The folks in Lubbock were great people, there's no question. Lubbock was a bigger place. Pullman is about thirty thousand people, and Lubbock was about two hundred twenty (thousand), but both of them have great airports. A lot more flights come out this direction between Spokane and stuff like that, you can get more direct flights out here, so even though it's smaller, maybe it's not quite as isolated."

— *Leach, comparing Lubbock, Texas, and Pullman, Washington*

"Anybody who wants to talk to Graham (Harrell) or Michael Crabtree, you can do it in their natural habitat in Lubbock, Texas. I recommend Love Field because DFW (Airport) can be a confusing mess. Love Field, about every hour, goes to Lubbock, Texas, where we have some great steak places, and we'd love to see you, and we all know you by your first names, so it'd be good to renew our friendship."

— *Leach, to reporters on not bringing his star players to the Big 12 media conference day in Dallas*

"I'm sincerely appreciative of your thoughtful gesture and may take you up on it. We are coming up fast on our season, and I might not have time to accept your invitation until December. I'm looking forward to meeting the good folks at DFW International Airport and American Airlines."

— *Leach, to DFW Airport officials after they sent him a letter offering the Leach family a complimentary flight to the facility on American Airlines and a steak dinner when they arrive*

"It was fun having a unique deal that no one else had. It's like keeping up with the Joneses. If one school goes out and buys a boat, you have to buy a boat, too."

— Leach, on the removal of Astroturf at Jones AT&T Stadium and replacing it with FieldTurf, 2006

"If you're slow on grass, you're still slow on turf. If you're fast, you're still fast. It's all relative."

— Leach, on whether teams needed to adjust to playing on Texas Tech's artificial playing surface

"One thing I've always liked about this place is you've got the great college atmosphere, but it's got a little bit of that NFL flavor with some characters mixed in. It's like a college atmosphere mixed with a David Lynch movie, so it's really pretty cool."

— Leach, on Texas Tech's Jones SBC/AT&T Stadium

"It's very savage to play in Lubbock. I would recommend everybody that can, try to avoid it. There have been scalpings, and there have been some people that quite simply just haven't returned. There are some people, unfortunately, based on the way the conference goes, that are going to have to come to our place. Sadly, I can't guarantee their safety or that things will necessarily go the way that they like."

— Leach, joking about Texas Tech's home field advantage

"It's got chainsaws, woodpeckers, people scratching on chalkboards, and all that so that players can't talk among themselves and they have to execute their plays nonverbally."

— Leach, on working out in Jones SBC/AT&T Stadium with an amped-up soundtrack blaring for a crowd-noise effect

"It would probably be on a scale with Woodstock, I would say, as far as being an historic event where people gather. It's kind of a statement for our generation, I think."

— Leach, describing the atmosphere at Washington State's Martin Stadium leading up to a showdown with eighth-ranked Stanford, 2015

"Acoustics are a funny thing. You know, the loudest stadium I've ever played in was forty-five thousand people at War Memorial Stadium in Little Rock, Arkansas. The entire thing is concrete. It's like dropping a ball bearing in your neighbor's basement. Just the whole thing echoes. Anything you say or do echoes five times. Well, five times forty-five thousand is almost 250,000. It's really loud."

— Leach

"I think we did pretty good on that. I think for the most part, noise is overrated. It probably contributed to some of the delays and the false starts. Outside of that, I don't think it's a gigantic factor. You hear about all of these noisy stadiums, Florida's like this, and LSU's like that, and A&M's like this. All of those players out there are a little tougher to contend with than the noise, and A&M's players were pretty tough this last week."

— Leach, on playing on the road at Texas A&M and a loud Kyle Field

"I think A&M might be the loudest in the conference. As far as a game-day environment, it's one of my favorites. There's all the pageantry with the (Corps of Cadets) march and stuff like that. In the conference, I'm not sure it's not the best game-day environment . . . outside of Jones SBC Stadium."

— Leach

"Well, it's not as loud as some, but it's not quiet, either. Plus, I hear they have a horse (mascot) now, too, so hopefully, we'll feel right at home."

— *Leach, on Texas Tech playing at Oklahoma State's Boone Pickens Stadium*

"You know the difference between a loud stadium and a less-loud stadium. Despite some of the really clever plays some people are trying to yell out and some clever insults, with a rare exception you don't hear them. You do hear the occasional one that's kind of clever, in the prank phone call kind of way. It just becomes noise and you are kind of absorbed in the game."

— *Leach*

"None of that spring break movie stuff, you know? No bullfights, no gambling, no donkeys, no vanilla extract, no piñatas, none of that stuff. Straight football. No switchblades."

— *Leach, when asked if he planned to take his team over the border to Ciudad Juarez for tourist attractions when Texas Tech played at UTEP*

"I know how loud the stadium is. It doesn't take too many people to get loud. And it's a cool atmosphere, a cool vibe. It's like football in middle of a Western. You're waiting for something, cowboys, Indians, outlaws, to come over the ridge. And the food in El Paso is great."

— *Leach, on his Washington State team being invited to play in the Sun Bowl in El Paso, 2015*

"I hope they have a big-time year in Springfield. Or Columbia. It's Columbia."

— *Leach, after Texas Tech lost to Missouri in Columbia, 41-10, 2007*

"It's incredible, it's one of the greatest game-day environments that I've ever been a part of. There's little old ladies with their children and grandchildren doing a variety of hand gestures letting you know just what they think of you exactly."

— *Leach, on playing LSU at Tiger Stadium*

"It's always tough in Austin. They're a good team. It's always — you know, I don't worry about the atmosphere quite as much as I do, you know, the Longhorn players and coaches and just the quality of the team."

— *Leach, on playing Texas at Darrell K. Royal Memorial Stadium in Austin*

"Ole Miss is a nice place and I'd like to vacation here. But I did not like having to play here. But it was a good win for our team."

— *Leach, after Texas Tech's 49-45 win over Ole Miss in Oxford, Mississippi, 2003*

"Sometimes I think our players can get sidetracked in, I don't know, the lovefest nature of our stadium. Our focus needs to be out there on the field. But we have incredible fans, and I really appreciate their participation making today what it was."

— *Leach, on the "distractions" of Washington State playing at home (Martin Stadium)*

"I was waiting for George Jetson and Elroy and the dog to come out and start doing some stuff and buzz around and do their thing. It's very impressive, and the quality they said it is, it is. It was fun."

— *Leach, on his impression of the new state-of-the-art Cowboys Stadium, where Tech defeated Baylor, 2009*

"I've never been to a bad one."

— *Leach, when asked his preference of bowl games*

"If you can think of a good angle for us, let me know. What about . . . win one for Sharon."

— *Leach, in noting that, although opponent California was the sentimental favorite against Texas Tech in the Holiday Bowl (San Diego), his wife Sharon went to high school there*

"I imagine it would, I don't know that for sure. Ever since they started naming bowls after corporations instead of flowers, fruits, and plants, I've lost track of how they do that exactly."

— *Leach, when asked if a Texas Tech upset of top-ranked Oklahoma would propel his team into a more prestigious bowl game, 2000*

"This is a demanding time. Everybody thinks you sit around, join hands, and sing 'Kumbaya.'"

— *Leach, on preparing for a bowl game when he was at Texas Tech*

"HE'S LIKE A FOLK HERO DOWN THERE. WE'RE HOPING WE'LL GET SOME NEW COUGAR FANS THAT ARE MIKE LEACH FANS WHO MIGHT HELP US FILL OUR ALLOTMENT AND FILL THE STADIUM."

— *Bill Moos, Washington State athletic director, on the Cougars playing Miami in the Sun Bowl in El Paso, Texas*

"There's a lot of great people in Texas, really, the Texas Tech fans and faithful were fantastic, just like Coug fans. Texas Tech hasn't paid me for 2009, the last season I worked (in Lubbock), so administratively, they've made some suspect decisions in the past. But the opportunity to connect with the state of Texas and bring what we have at WSU, the exciting team we have — I'm excited to bring the two worlds back together."

— Leach, on returning to Texas with his
Washington State team to play in the Sun Bowl, 2015

"I didn't really keep track of it. I figured we'd win this one and go from there."

— Leach, when asked about Washington State's
ending a twelve-year bowl victory drought with
a 20-14 win over Miami in the 2015 Sun Bowl

"I've only been to Philly a couple of times before — I've always liked it from a distance. I always wondered why that was. Was it the good food? I'm thinking, Yes, it's good food, but that's not exactly it. If the fans don't like the way things are going football-wise, they throw snowballs, which I like, because I think fans should be involved in the game and should have a little bit of passion in regard to what's going on."

— Leach, in his acceptance speech for the
George Munger Coach of the Year award presented
by the Maxwell Football Club in Philadelphia, 2008

"I took my family and it was like the movie *European Vacation*. It was the wife, the kids, the frequent-flier miles . . . the whole thing. It's one of those things that ten years from now they'll say what great fun they had, but right now they were [complaining] about all of the walking, the tough stuff, and the food. It was a great time, and we covered a lot of ground in a sensory-overload kind of a deal."

— ***Leach***, *after a summer vacation to England, Scotland, and France*

"I annoyed my entire family by going through Hampton Court and the Tower of London by reading everything. I read everything and they were very irritated wanting to go get something to eat. The worst thing about it was kind of dark reading it because they wanted to preserve the lettering [on the plaques]."

— ***Leach***, *on the family's European vacation*

"Those of you thinking of gift items, you know, you can perhaps get a Catwoman outfit for your wife. And then there's some cool brass knuckles with blades on it and things of that nature."

— ***Leach***, *on visiting the Batman museum and gift shop at Warner Bros. Studios during Pac-12 Media Day*

"Typically it's a beach or an island, where I try to avoid the resort aspect of it . . . not some city where you wander around and have appetizers and go to museums."

— ***Leach***, *on his ideal vacation*

"What I like about Club Med is it's all-inclusive, and so you call them up, and once you cut the deal it's done, and they're scattered all over the place and they've got a bunch of tropical locations. Your quarter isn't fancy. It's basically kinda dorm room-like, which I don't mind, because you're going to be outside the whole time. The food's awesome, and then the other thing is you'll go there and the other people are from all over the world. You'll hear a bunch of different languages spoken and stuff like that, and occasionally there'll be some who don't want to speak English to you, but heck, you're not going to know them that well anyway, so just keep talking to them and eventually they'll break down and speak with you."

— Leach

"I always wondered why I wasn't the fan of Las Vegas that a lot of people are. I think the reason is that Las Vegas is a mall and I don't really care for malls. It may not have clothes and may not have Foot Locker and Orange Julius and all that other stuff, which are great places, but it's a mall of slot machines and blackjack tables and the rest. It's sort of like milling around in a mall — when I come back from Las Vegas I feel like I've spent three days in the mall."

— Leach

"He always has to drive. No matter who's there, he always has to drive. . . . When I was a kid, he'd say, 'Let's just go for a drive.' Well, 'Let's just go for a drive' was like two hours. There wouldn't be any fifteen-minute drives. You could always see it coming because he'd say, 'Let's go stretch my eyes.' . . . I'm the opposite, I want anybody to drive, but me."

— Leach, recalling his childhood and his father's "driving"

"I've always thought that the French (people) were a little misunderstood. Even the snotty ones are odd enough to be interesting."

— *Leach*

"One year we went to New York and New Jersey. Basically, New Jersey has good players, but bad football. They got a lot of people and some of them can play, but overall, my opinion, they start the season late and end it early. Statistically, they send a lot of players to the NFL. They tend to have smaller schools population-wise. There's a bunch of teams I could play on. There's guys out there who are great players (in high school) and turn out to be good ones, but based on competition, you won't get a feel for it. I didn't think I could evaluate New Jersey. Some of it was just experience with the leagues there. If you have a feel for quality, you can make a better judgment."

— *Leach, recalling a recruiting trip to the Northeast as an assistant coach*

"Craps is the most analytical game, but that's kind of a math question, and I didn't really go to Las Vegas to do math."

— *Leach, on vacationing in Las Vegas*

"It's eerily similar to the other times I've been in Texas."

— *Leach, when asked what it was like to return to Texas (El Paso) for the Sun Bowl, 2015*

4
No Injuries, No Excuses

"We have a whole bunch of people that are going to go out there and practice and play and achieve things. . . on the field. So I am more than willing to talk about them, and those are the people that need to be discussed and recognized. We don't have any alibis for injuries. Teams that sit and talk about injuries all the time provide themselves with an excuse for not being successful or as successful as they might be. We are not going to provide that for anybody — excuses or alibis for underachievement — so that is another reason (injuries are not mentioned). The other reason, I am not interested in a guy all of a sudden that generates attention just because he is injured. And then the other thing, well, I just think it's journalism at its lowest level, if you are so uncreative that you can't come up with a story or devise a story or find something newsworthy outside of any injury. I mean, 'Oh, all these folks are injured.' Well, hey, that's not a story and a chimpanzee can write that. So I don't want to provide or aid any of that."

— **Leach**

Mike Leach doesn't discuss injuries, so we'll just leave it at that.

"We've got lots of injuries, and we picked up more (Saturday). But we knew that could be a problem going in. You just have to work with it."

— Leach, after six Texas Tech starters suffered injuries, 2000 (A rare injury quote before the coach implemented a "no injury" comment policy in 2003)

"Injuries come as they come, and you just have to deal with them. Most of ours have been under odd circumstances, and, other than that, we've stayed pretty healthy."

— Leach, 2001

"I don't think he really got hurt. They stuck a brace on him as a precautionary thing. He kinda does that little skip . . . I'm sure you've seen him do it. He did the skip, and he skipped different than he skipped before."

— Leach, on a knee injury Texas Tech quarterback B. J. Symons suffered during a touchdown celebration against Iowa State, 2003

"They are going to look at him running around and gauge it just on how he runs around. He was running around yesterday; he looked pretty decent. I don't know where it's at. I'm sure that somebody is going to be poking on stuff, 'Does this hurt,' and things of that nature, and reach a determination on whether he's healthy. But he is running around pretty decently."

— Leach, on injured Texas Tech receiver Anton Paige, 2001

"Handle it however you want, but you're not getting anything (injury information) out of us. If you do (from staff), I'll fire 'em, and if you do out of a player, I'll cut 'em."

> — **Leach**, *announcing his new no-injury policy to media after being upset about reports of an injury to Texas Tech defensive end Adell Duckett, 2003*

"This is the only place that I've ever been in eighteen years of coaching where we had stories that related to injuries on three networks, a couple of newspapers, and the radio. There's obviously an obsession that exists outside this football program with it, so we're not going to do anything to contribute to the addiction that relates to that."

> — **Leach**, *to the Lubbock media*

"I don't know why you'd think otherwise. Of course he's going to play. We're having a game; B. J. plays in games."

> — **Leach**, *when asked if 'injured' Texas Tech quarterback B. J. Symons was going to play in an upcoming game, 2003*

"Well, I expect everybody to be back since there hasn't been an injury around here in five years or whenever it started. I don't know why this week would be any different. And so, you know, we'll go out and practice and see what happens."

> — **Leach**, *when asked if "injured" Texas Tech quarterback Taylor Potts was going to play in an upcoming game, 2009*

"The Red Raiders haven't had any injuries happening. It's been kind of remarkable. To the best of my knowledge, he'll (cornerback L.A. Reed) play well . . . like gangbusters."

> — *Leach, on a Texas Tech player whose ankle was immobilized in a protective boot during practice*

"Amazingly, for over two years we've been 100 percent healthy. There hasn't been so much as a hangnail in two and a half years. So anything that has to do with health or injury, there's no excuses to hide behind here. Because this team, in every game, we're as healthy as we can be."

> — *Leach, as the 2014 season began at Washington State*

"He's doing fabulously well, and he's a great member of our team, and we continue to look forward to his success."

> — *Leach, when asked about Taylor Potts's status after the Texas Tech quarterback was released from the hospital*

"They're incredibly healthy and have the strength of ten vikings."

> — *Leach, on injured Texas Tech wide receiver Detron Lewis and defensive end Rajon Henley, 2009*

"He's ridiculously healthy. He's one of those guys that Tony the Tiger would be proud of to be in a commercial and have him eat cereal and everything, you know what I mean?"

> — *Leach, when asked about the status of injured Washington State quarterback Jeff Tuel, 2012*

"Healthy as can be, we rested him in the second half."

> — *Leach, when asked in a postgame interview about Washington State quarterback Luke Falk, who was carted off the field with a head injury, 2015*

"Somebody is going to play that position no matter what, and the last thing we're going to do is create a distraction for our team and sing the blues and act like somehow we're working our way out of a hole because someone else is playing that position. Because the other person playing the position may be just as good or better than the last one. And I, quite frankly, don't understand coaches that are constantly talking about injuries because, to me, it smells of hiding behind trying to generate an excuse in case they need one after the fact, if the game doesn't go the way they hope it does."

> — *Leach*

"I would still refuse. I would still be very elusive on it. It would also violate the HIPAA (Health Insurance Portability and Accountability Act) law, which would be interesting to me if the Pac-12 could get that law overturned. It's nobody's business. If some kid doesn't want you to know, why should you? No, I still wouldn't tell."

— *Leach, on the idea that the Pac-12 would require teams to provide an official injury report*

"Well, it's pretty much out there. He broke his ankle. . . . You can go read that report and then go ahead and ask that guy, and then whatever you draw from that, that would be great. . . . The whole ankle. Well, the tibula [*sic*] and the fibula are in the ankle, you see. Here, let me show you (Leach said, placing his leg onto the conference table). Big bone, little bone. Both of them."

— *Leach, at a press conference, trying to describe a season-ending injury (broken leg or ankle?) to Washington State quarterback Connor Halliday, 2014*

"I'm thinking, isn't this sort of like breast implants — why don't you get both done? Maybe he'll get the other one done later."

— *Leach, after Halliday told him that a rod inserted into his broken ankle had made that ankle stronger than the other one*

5
Nick the Quarterback and Others

"He says that if just anybody could play quarterback in this system, he'd recruit a girl from the Swedish Bikini Team because she'd be a lot more fun to watch."

— **Cody Hodges**, Texas Tech quarterback, on Leach's Air Raid offense

Tim Couch, Josh Heupel, Kliff Kingsbury, B. J. Symons, Sonny Cumbie, Cody Hodges, Graham Harrell, Taylor Potts, Connor Halliday, and Luke Falk are among the many outstanding quarterbacks that Mike Leach has coached over the years.

As offensive coordinator at Kentucky, Leach tutored Couch, who went on to be the number-one pick in the 1999 NFL Draft. As offensive coordinator at Oklahoma, Leach recruited and then oversaw the progress of Heupel.

The next six quarterbacks on the above list played, in chronological order, for Leach at Texas Tech, seemingly breaking each other's records each succeeding year.

Despite setting numerous records, those quarterbacks never received the amount of national recognition and NFL interest they deserved, according to Leach. Instead, they were viewed by many as merely interchangeable parts in Leach's Air Raid offense quarterback "system."

In one of Leach's more unusual psychological ploys, he renamed struggling Texas Tech quarterback Taylor Potts "Nick" during the 2009 season in honor of a tough player he admired — former Kansas line-backer Nick Reid.

Leach even had "Nick" stitched onto the back of Potts's jersey. The coach said he "always felt like (Reid) personified what a football player is and what a football player should be." As Potts was going through his tough times, Leach said, "We decided all our players, we'd like them to be more like Nick, and led by Nick would be even better. We figured it wouldn't hurt us to have a Nick, so now we do."

"Yes, I would think so. I would think so, and it was his idea, too, while we're on the subject because I'm going to get blamed for this. I guarantee you. As the expression on his relatives and his girlfriend's face changes, on some level I'm going to get blamed for this. But for the record, it was his idea to have it on the jersey. I named him Nick."

— Leach, when asked if 'Nick' would stay on Taylor Potts's jersey the rest of the season

"If (Texas Tech quarterback) B. J. Symons is a product of the system, then he's not getting any of those touchdown passes and all those yards. That means our coaching staff is. That would also mean we could go down to 7-11 and get the clerk behind the counter and let him play quarterback."

— Leach, on the "system"

"He had that whole John Wayne quality. The ultimate dust-and-tumbleweeds-coming- from-Abilene, quiet kind of guy. Even now he kind of is."

— Leach, on Texas Tech quarterback Taylor Potts of Abilene, Texas

"He looks like Kenny Stabler and acts like Bart Starr."

— Leach, on Potts

"I don't think Potts ever got in a rhythm. I don't know if he tried to make too much happen, but he looked slow and statue-like."

— Leach, on a poor performance by Potts in Texas Tech's 52-30 loss to Texas A&M, 2009

"It wasn't one of those deals where you're introducing him to pretty girls and taking him for a steak dinner. I didn't have a lot of furniture in my office, so we basically sat cross-legged on the floor watching video and talking until he said he'd rather be a Sooner than go to Utah State."

— Leach, on recruiting quarterback Josh Heupel when Leach was offensive coordinator at Oklahoma

"He really does have good pocket presence. It's not just quick feet or how fast the guy is. It's sort of instinctual."

— Leach, on Texas Tech quarterback Cody Hodges, 2005

"As far as yelling goes, I think you reserve yelling for when you're not getting great effort. Anybody in the world can give great effort. I think that's required of everybody. If you're not getting great effort, I think you don't hesitate to get their attention. If you're getting great effort out of somebody, but they're just doing it incorrectly, I think it's your job to teach him. I don't think effort was his problem; I think more relaxation was his problem. I think he needed to relax."

— Leach, on how he handles players, after a poor game by Texas Tech quarterback B. J. Symons, 2003

"You can't really have a quarterback that gets rattled, (and) I've never had luck with a dumb guy. I've had a bunch of good quarterbacks, but (Harrell) really is comfortable with the whole package and getting us into the best play."

— Leach, on Texas Tech quarterback Graham Harrell, 2007

"First of all, Kliff's (Kingsbury) year, no one was even sure he could play quarterback anyway. Well, then, it turns out he can. And then it turns out he has a pretty good year. Then the perception is as well, it will be impossible to replace him. That's probably the last of the great quarterbacks. Woe is Texas Tech.

"Then, as it turns out, to the delight of everyone, B. J. Symons could play quarterback as well. Then B. J. leaves and it's like, of course [Sonny Cumbie] will be a great quarterback. This guy will walk on water right out of the gates. So they go from 'It's impossible' to, 'Of course, he's going to be an NFL Hall of Famer' the day he steps out onto the field. I guess that goes with the territory. I think with B. J., they were pleasantly surprised, and if Joe Namath were here, there would be a certain level of disappointment just because now there's a level of expectation. Both of those quarterbacks are tough acts to follow and everyone tends to remember their last game instead of their first three games. [Cumbie's] right on pace and he's doing fine."

— *Leach, on criticism of Texas Tech quarterback Sonny Cumbie, 2004*

"Kliff is the All-American boy, while B. J. is kind of punk rock."

— *Leach, comparing quarterbacks Kliff Kingsbury and B. J. Symons*

"He got a lot of pressure, but he generated some for himself, too. There were a couple of them where he'd go back there and run in a circle, run in a circle, and look up and then there's two guys there. I wasn't real cranked about that. I wanted him to throw the ball and hit some fat guy in the stands. That didn't consistently happen. We had a conversation on that."

— *Leach, on the scrambling of walk-on quarterback Steven Sheffield, who, in his first career start, led Texas Tech to a 31-10 victory over Nebraska*

"He got knocked down more times than he should've, but that's part of what quarterbacks do. I mean, if you play football, you get hit. I think he's fine, and I think that's all part of it. We certainly would rather he not get hit, but if he does get hit, he'll just have to get back up and go, you know?"

— Leach, on Cody Hodges, after a hard-hitting game against Kansas, in which the Texas Tech quarterback was sacked five times, 2005

"One of his best qualities is he tries to make a lot happen. One of his worst qualities is he tries to make a lot happen."

— Leach, on Washington State quarterback Connor Halliday

"I think he's just sorting it out quicker. He's not pondering the mysteries of life; I think he's going out there and reacting quicker, and it's helped him quite a bit."

— Leach, on Washington State quarterback Luke Falk's improved decision-making

"There's no real secret to it. I mean, you try to figure out who is the best one, and you play 'em."

— Leach, when asked how he chooses a starting quarterback

"Clearly, he's one of the best quarterbacks in the entire nation. You might be rooting for your guy, and I don't care what you think. He's better than your guy is."

— Leach, on Washington State quarterback Connor Halliday

"I'd have to say Jeff would be a little more like Stonewall Jackson. Gets hold of the play, attacks from different angles. The cavalry is over here, no, we're here. He's not afraid to split the force. Travis is more of a Ulysses S. Grant guy. He's in the trenches, and if it requires bombarding for a month, he's fully prepared to do it. He's going to bombard them till they bust, provided he keeps his pads low."

*— **Leach**, when asked to which military leaders he would compare Washington State players Jeff Tuel and Travis Long*

"For all I know, he had flip-flops on. But he went down there and popped the thing in front of everybody. What got our attention is he didn't take any extra steps, and it went straight up. It's not like he warmed up. He wasn't up there in the stands with some little kicking net and a remedial shoe and all that stuff."

*— **Leach**, on Matt Williams, who came out of the stands in a halftime kicking contest and later walked on and became Texas Tech's starting placekicker, 2008*

"Somebody on a campus can kick. Somebody on campus can snap, and so it goes. Sometimes you got to turn over some stones."

*— **Leach**, noting that college campuses probably have plenty of talented students who played high school sports but weren't recruited*

"I look at it this way: This university has twenty-four thousand people. Out of twelve thousand males, approximately, there's X number of football players, and of those football players, somebody can long snap. But what happens a lot of times with a long snapper is he'll play some other position and may not be a college-level guy at other positions, but is a long snapper. But people don't necessarily chase around and scholarship long-snappers until they've proven themselves for a couple years. They sort of assume, well, nobody's interested or cares. I don't know how many guys on this campus can long snap, but I promise you, there's at least twenty people on this campus who can long snap. That doesn't mean they want to. But there's at least twenty guys on this campus who can long snap."

— **Leach**, *after taking out an ad in the Washington State student newspaper seeking a long snapper*

"You know how weird kickers are. Andrew's no exception to that, but he's certainly not as weird as some of them, and I think that alone transcends him above the group."

— **Leach**, *on Washington State kicker Andrew Furney, 2013*

"We're concerned now, but he's gonna be really good. The thing is, if you think back to all of them (previous kickers), they all had a developmental period. They've all gone through some growing pains. In his case, he works real hard, great work ethic there. He's not one of those guys that pouts in between. If they do, you gotta slap the pouting out of them."

— **Leach**, *on struggling Texas Tech kicker Donnie Carona, 2008*

"If you've seen that Foghorn Leghorn cartoon, Wes was like the chicken hawk. He was shorter than everybody, one of those barrel-chested guys with thick ankles. I was thinking, 'This fella is pretty sure of himself.' He had this steely-eyed stare, this look that said, 'I can whip all their asses.'"

*— **Leach**, recalling seeing receiver Wes Welker at Texas Tech's first team meeting, 2000*

"Well, Wes had the huge punt return, and I thought that once we got him showered off, we're going to have everyone hug him."

*— **Leach**, when asked about the play of Wes Welker, 2002*

"A great player, he is a great example of what a player should be. Michael Crabtree has had the ability to adjust and get all of his talents to the surface quickly. One of the reasons he has is just because he is an incredibly dedicated, hard-working guy. He is also a real clear-minded and focused person."

*— **Leach***

"Michael Crabtree has been more successful as a receiver than that guy has as a coach. Michael isn't a diva; he's too shy to be like that. My definition of a diva is someone who's loud and self-absorbed. Michael is the furthest thing from loud that I've seen. Let's see how all those non-divas do up in Cleveland this year."

*— **Leach**, responding to comments made by Cleveland Browns coach Mark Mangini and other team officials that the former Tech receiver was a diva*

"He's got kind of a deep, stately voice and sounds kind of like a college professor and uses those kinds of words. He's a very intelligent guy. One of the biggest things people don't know about him is his demeanor and how articulate he is. When you talk to him it's not even like the normal guy on the street. It's got a weird formal quality to it. He just needs a pipe or something."

— ***Leach***, *on Texas Tech receiver Jarrett Hicks*

"WE KIND OF KNEW ABOUT HIM, HE'S REALLY GOOD. [L. A.] REED MADE A NICE CATCH, TOO, AND THEN YOU'VE GOT THOSE OTHER TWO LITTLE RUGRATS RUNNING AROUND THERE CATCHING BALLS ALL OVER THE PLACE AND YOU CAN'T STOP THEM."

— ***Mike Price***, *University of Texas at El Paso coach, on Texas Tech receivers Michael Crabtree and "rugrats" Eric Morris and Danny Amendola, after a 45-31 UTEP loss to Tech*

"HE CALLS ME THE 'EVIL ELF' BECAUSE HE HAS ALL THESE DIFFERENT THINGS: ELVES ARE SMALL, THEY'RE GENERALLY PRETTY MEAN, AND THEY CORNER WELL. THEY'RE GOOD WITH A DAGGER — HE GOES ON AND ON ABOUT HOW ELVES HAVE DIFFERENT TRAITS, AND HE THINKS THAT I FIT THE TRAITS OF AN ELF. HE THINKS THAT I DO WELL WITH THE FOOTBALL IN MY HANDS AND CALLS THE FOOTBALL MY DAGGER."

— ***Eric Morris***, *Texas Tech wide receiver, on being nicknamed "Elf" by Leach, 2008*

"Besides the obvious size thing, he looks like an elf. I mean, just look at him. We ought to play him in a green jersey. He'd do it, too. They need to make a movie about him, kind of like *Bad Santa*, except it's called *Bad Elf*, because he's not a warm, cuddly, fuzzy-feeling elf. He's kind of evil and sinister."

— ***Leach***, *on Eric Morris*

"He's really got the ability to get open. That's the one unique thing about receivers is that there's fast ones, slow ones, tall ones, short ones, fat ones, skinny ones. The thing of it is, if you can get open and catch the ball, you can play receiver. He's good at getting open and catching the ball."

— ***Leach***, *on Texas Tech wide receiver Trey Haverty, 2004*

"We make dreams come true around here if somebody is willing to work hard to make it happen. We were blessed when Torres came to our team, and he's made the most of his opportunity as it's happened."

— ***Leach***, *on Texas Tech receiver Alex Torres, a transfer who worked his way into being one of the team's top receivers, 2009*

"You've got to keep fast guys going fast, so they keep going fast."

— ***Leach***, *on speedy receivers*

"HIS BIG DEAL IS OUR RECEIVERS USING THEIR HANDS TO GET OFF A PRESS OR TO GET OPEN, RUNNING A ROUTE. AND OUR RECEIVERS HAVE A HARD TIME WITH THAT SOMETIMES OR WE HAVE A HARD TIME WITH PRESS COVERAGE. SO HE'D SAY, 'GABE MARKS, HE DOESN'T USE HIS HANDS, SO THE NEXT GENERATION, HIS SONS AND HIS SONS' SONS ARE GOING TO END UP LOOKING LIKE T-REXES WITHOUT ANY ARMS, BECAUSE HE REFUSES TO USE THEM.' SO, IF YOU WANT YOUR SONS TO HAVE ARMS AND DO THINGS WITH HIS HANDS, THEN *YOU* SHOULD USE *YOUR* HANDS."

— **Connor Halliday**, *Washington State quarterback,*
recalling a Leach teaching moment in practice

"I think focus. I think from the day he got here he was always very focused, very driven, worked very hard. Didn't allow distractions, which I think one good thing about him is, he does it naturally. I don't know what all his hobbies are, but I think all his hobbies involve something football-related. Because every time I see him, he's either thinking or doing football. He's not one of those guys after a good play or a bad play has a whole lot of dialogue."

— **Leach**, *when asked what makes Washington*
State's River Cracraft such an outstanding receiver

"Well, he was in a different kind of shape. I mean, he was built like a Saturday morning cartoon character . . . he was all chiseled up. He's like one of those figurines your mom bought you as a child that you may still have. I don't know, but it looked like Vince. He didn't have a monster face, but it looked like Vince. The biggest thing is he's more fluid now, he's down to probably 220 pounds, and a lot more fluid and quicker and a lot more precise in his technique."

— **Leach**, *on Washington State receiver Vince Mayle getting into shape*

"I remember when he first used to go out there, he reminded me of a baby moose. I mean, I don't know how many moose are in Texas, but there's a lot in Wyoming. He's a really strong, physical, explosive guy. And he's getting to the place where he can really put the power and finesse together in a pretty good fashion. Well, he's getting antlers now, you know."

— *Leach, on the maturity of Texas Tech receiver Joel Filani, 2006*

"He needs to be like those grizzly bears in Yellowstone Park that start tipping over dumpsters and throwing garbage out of them at the lodges. Next practice, we're going to stick a dumpster in front of him."

— *Leach, saying that Washington State tight end Andrei Lintz has good hands, but needs to use them more in downfield blocking and shedding coverage, 2012*

"We don't entirely know what we have with him. We're looking forward to seeing. I think he's got real soft hands and catches the ball real well."

— *Leach, on Texas Tech receiver Adam James, 2007*

"Ed didn't like showing up and studying at places I felt like he needed to and like the academic people asked him to. So he can study on the fifty-yard line. We'll take baby steps, and if he does good studying out there, we'll decide if we're going to actually let him practice. If somehow he fails to do that, then that'll be the last we see of Easy Ed."

— *Leach, on Texas Tech receiver Ed Britton, who was told to study at a desk at midfield in the stadium in snowy, cold weather during the off-season, 2009*

Luke Falk of Washington State is the latest in a long line of outstanding quarterbacks coached by Mike Leach.

"I think that Dylan's done a good job. He's steady also. One thing is Dylan's got pretty good feet. He's got better feet, I think, than he sometimes gets credit for."

— ***Leach***, *on Texas Tech offensive lineman Dylan Gandy, 2004*

"Brandon Carter, with regard to hair and style, is like a woman that works at a beauty parlor. There's a lot of change. The new thing comes out, there's some experimentation. 'Let's change the color of it today. I saw in a magazine, I saw this, so let's see how this looks.' He feels like he needs a piece of the action, and I say, why shouldn't he?"

— ***Leach***, *on Texas Tech offensive lineman Brandon Carter's unique hairstyle and face make-up, 2008*

"He's got the highest test score on our team, and he's a ridiculously articulate person. I remember he hadn't had German or anything, and he had the class, so he was taking something like German II because it fit his schedule better. And then, of course, he did real well."

— Leach, on Brandon Carter

"I think it's impressive. Duncan's kind of emerged last year doing some real good things. Hopefully, he can continue to develop this year and continue his community service, but keep track of his community service here on the field, too."

— Leach, on Texas Tech linebacker Brian Duncan,
who was recognized for participating in
community service events in Lubbock, 2008

"Shannon Woods is one of my favorite running backs in the whole world. As a matter of fact, I probably like Shannon Woods more than any ten players on any other team."

— Leach, although later in his career the
Texas Tech running back would land in Leach's doghouse

"I don't think he competed very hard. Somebody asked me if stats from last year register for anything. Well, they don't because you don't get any points out of them and you don't get any results out of them this year. You have good results, you compete, and you play hard, it puts you where it puts you. He is where he is."

— Leach, on demoting Shannon Woods to third-team, 2007

"The doghouse pretty well ended when we started spring and he competed hard. He always has had the ability to be really polished. When's he's on his A-game, he blocks as good as anybody in the league. When he's doing all the little things right, he's pretty good."

*— **Leach**, on Woods climbing out of the doghouse after not playing in the final four games of the previous season*

"He's been a host on several recruit weekends and does a very good job of evaluating various steaks and steak places and the places where we eat on the visit. I've asked his advice on that type of thing before, and he can you give a very thorough and specific answer on what he likes. I'm not sure that he perhaps shouldn't run his own steak place at some point in time. He's very sharp at it."

*— **Leach**, on asking for restaurant advice from Texas Tech freshman running back Kobey Lewis*

"I don't consider him a newcomer anymore. He's been repping a lot and has a grasp of what we're doing. He knows how to register for classes, so he's not a maintenance item."

*— **Leach**, on Texas Tech freshman wide receiver Thomas Bachman, who enrolled at midterm and joined the team for spring drills*

"Certainly, Vincent's as talented as any running back on the team. Those two guys are more experienced than he is, and as you look at your talent and juggle it around you try to figure out how you can spend all your money, so to speak, rather than keep it in your wallet. So we're trying to figure out a way to spend Vincent for the whole cause."

— *Leach, on moving Texas Tech running back Vincent Meeks to the secondary*

"Kristoff Williams was doing some very valiant and gallant things . . . it's remarkably highly classified. If I were to tell you, I'd jeopardize world peace, so I'm not going to."

— *Leach, when asked why a Washington State receiver was missing from the team for a game, 2014*

"Keep in mind, recruits will go places because they like the color of somebody's jersey or they always use that team when they play Madden or because their sixteen-year-old girlfriend thinks that they ought to go to this place or that place."

— *Leach, on the inexact science of recruiting*

"There (are) too many cooks in the kitchen on recruiting. I think it's a constant — people get social media faster than they ever have, more than they ever have. Within a split second, something can deliver some type of an impression in somebody's mind."

— *Leach, on the difficulty in gaining firm commitments from recruits*

"So far, the recruiting class is shaping up, they're always a little different than you have on paper right now. They could improve a little or depreciate a little; it just depends what happens because the eighteen-year-old mind works mysteriously."

— Leach

"He's big and likes to hit things. He's our kind of guy."

— Leach, on 6-8, 350-pound freshman offensive lineman Cody O'Connell, 2013

"If you get them in the weight room — you need to get to the point where they marinate in there a couple of years. . . . Their feet get better, their strength gets better. It's a man position, and, over time, you kind of develop man muscles rather than kid muscles."

— Leach, on developing young offensive linemen

"Those (offensive linemen) are the most important positions. I don't want to take anything away from our quarterbacks, receivers, DBs, and our linebackers, but it's hard to replace those guys. Part of it is because God didn't make very many of them to begin with."

— Leach

"I don't ask (recruiting services) what to call on third-and-long, so I don't really care what they think. If a player's got (a rating of) five stars, I might think he's terrible. I probably got minus three stars for recruiting Wes Welker. At some point, you switch on the film and do you like him? Darrell Royal (legendary Texas coach) was one of the first guys that said never be afraid to recruit somebody that nobody else is recruiting."

— Leach

"He is a good Scandinavian guy. I like him."

— *Leach, on Big 12 commissioner Kevin Weiberg*

"FROM WATCHING THE VIDEO, IT LOOKS LIKE COACH LEACH WENT TO THE UNDERWORLD AND RECRUITED A BUNCH OF LYCANS TO RUN UP AND DOWN THE FIELD."

— *Bruce Barnum, Portland State coach, 2015*

"The thing most people don't understand about Bob is what a great guy he is to work for. Most head coaches love to talk. It's just their nature, but with him, it's not like he's Mr. Chairman of the Board or anything. He's unique because he's a listener. He's interested in what others on the staff have to offer. He taught me that, so I'll listen up to a point, but pretty soon I'll tell them all to shut up because I like to talk."

— *Leach, on University of Oklahoma coach Bob Stoops; Leach was offensive coordinator under Stoops for a year.*

"I looked up and saw this coat that said Texas A&M right after getting off the train. I must have looked terrible, yet he looked fresh as a daisy. I don't know how he does it."

— *Leach, recalling bumping into Texas A&M coach R. C. Slocum at Houston's Intercontinental Airport while the two were recruiting*

"If I go against Jeff, I wouldn't want to be involved with playing. I'd try to get in a term-paper contest."

— *Leach, on Texas Tech playing California and coach Jeff Tedford in the Holiday Bowl. Tedford played college football; Leach did not.*

"He is a friend of mine, and anybody that you have slumber parties with on the floor of the University of Oklahoma athletic complex outside your office, you know pretty well. We slept in our offices when we first got there, so there would be nights of coffee and microwave popcorn and film until Howard Stern came on."

> — *Leach, on his friendship with Mark Mangino,*
> *with whom Leach coached at Oklahoma*

"Playing against all these guys is the same as playing against anybody else because you're a little preoccupied with their players and their team. . . . There's no memory lane, there's no misty moment on the sideline, 'Oh, my gosh, good old Rich is over there.' None of that exists because there's all these Arizona Wildcats running around fast as can be, chasing around trying to tackle all of your guys and trying to disrupt your defense, so you're pretty preoccupied with that. Rich's a good guy, and so I'll see him, and we'll probably hang out some in the off-season."

> — *Leach, on playing against Arizona*
> *coach and good friend Rich Rodriguez*

"If I had been hired at the University of Alaska, Sonny Dykes would have been there if I could have gotten him up there."

> — *Leach, on one of his first hires at Texas Tech. Dykes,*
> *a son of Spike Dykes, was an assistant at Kentucky,*
> *where he and Leach had coached together a few years earlier.*

"They're all pretty sharp guys. You know, they're not yellers and hand-clappers."

> — *Leach, on his coaching tree, which includes the*
> *likes of Art Briles, Dana Holgorsen, Sonny Dykes,*
> *Kliff Kingsbury, Seth Littrell, and Lincoln Riley*

"Because I'm younger than those guys. . . . I got into coaching to coach. Otherwise, you're just a handshaker."

> — *Leach, on why he calls his own offensive*
> *plays, unlike some veteran head coaches*

"It was like meeting Marshal Dillon. Bobby has a huge presence. He commands attention, like someone from the Old West who can handle any situation. I liked being around Bobby, just in case those qualities would rub off."

> — *Leach, on meeting former Lubbock Monterey High School baseball coach Bobby Moegle for the first time. During Moegle's forty-year tenure at Monterey, his teams won four state titles and 1,115 games.*

"He's clearly one of the great organizers in the history of America. There's a weird combination of coming up with good ideas and getting them accomplished, and he's always been able to do that."

> — *Leach, on meeting businessman Donald Trump*

"One thing I've always admired about Spike Dykes is every time I talk to him, he's really happy. He's got the whole week situated out down at Horseshoe Bay, loving life, the whole thing. Most coaches don't do that. They hang on forever or they really struggle with retirement. They retire, but they're not happy. I guess my hope would be I would be able to do it like Spike."

> — *Leach, on his predecessor at Texas Tech and retirement*

6
Blowing the Whistle

"It's important to have good officiating at all levels, so if that means write your congressman, then you may want to consider that."

— **Leach**, after several critical penalties
against Texas Tech in a game with Oklahoma, 2001

No matter how questionable a call might be, football coaches know they aren't supposed to publicly criticize officiating crews. If they dare to, the risk includes a fine /reprimand/suspension from the powers that be.

But that didn't deter Mike Leach, whose principles won out over Big 12 Conference policy after Texas Tech's 59-43 loss to Texas in Austin in 2007.

In postgame remarks, he blasted the officials, using such terms as "incompetence" and "bias" while "condemning the crew."

Leach was particularly upset by the fact that the referee just happened to be a resident of Austin, Texas. And he was specifically upset with three calls, including two that disallowed Texas Tech touchdowns in the third quarter. The first score was overruled when replays showed the ball bounced off the turf in the end zone. On the next play, Tech had another touchdown pass negated by a holding penalty; Leach observed that a late hit should have been called against the Longhorns.

Big 12 commissioner Dan Beebe levied a record $10,000 fine and reprimand to Leach over the comments. But the Tech coach got the last laugh when a group of his supporters raised $5,000 to help pay the fine; the money was used to purchase holiday hams to feed needy people in Lubbock.

"I think it's disturbing that Austin residents are involved in this. People work too hard, too long, there's too much money invested in these games to allow that. . . . Am I condemning the crew? Hell, yeah, I'm condemning the crew. Unless this can change, the Big 12 Conference needs to take a serious look at having out-of-conference officials officiate the Texas Tech-Texas games and perhaps other games where there is proven to be a bias by officiating. It's unfortunate, and does the bowl picture enter into it? I don't know. Does the money enter into it? I don't know. It may be incompetence, bias, I don't know. Maybe it's something as simple as guys sitting over the water cooler at their office in Austin talking about the great game they're going to see — and then perhaps a preconceived notion develops as to how it's going to come out."

— *Leach, blasting the officiating, after the 59-43 loss to Texas in Austin, 2007*

"COACH LEACH'S PUBLIC STATEMENTS CALLED INTO QUESTION THE INTEGRITY AND COMPETENCE OF GAME OFFICIALS AND THE CONFERENCE'S OFFICIATING PROGRAM. ACCORDINGLY, THE SERIOUSNESS OF THIS VIOLATION WARRANTS A PUBLIC REPRIMAND AND THE LARGEST FINE ISSUED TO DATE BY THE CONFERENCE."

— *Dan Beebe, Big 12 commissioner*

"Made my feelings known already, so I don't have a reaction. . . . We've broke records around here before. We're used to breaking records."

— *Leach, reacting to his Beebe-levied fine*

"I'd almost need an attorney to figure out whether I'm supposed to answer that or not. Suffice it to say, referring to nothing even remotely related to officiating, I think as far as how we do instant replay maybe ought to be looked at, maybe other systems looked at."

*— **Leach**, when asked if he preferred there be no replay*

"I'm not allowed to comment on officiating. But those that looked at it or have a copy of the game . . . certainly they're gonna arrive at various opinions. This, after all, is America. And I'd encourage them to do so."

*— **Leach**, on the officiating, after a 35-31 loss to Texas, 2006*

"I certainly received some 'cyclical' this weekend, and not just from the University of Texas, either. Some 'cyclical' things I'm not entitled to comment on."

*— **Leach**, when asked whether the*
Big 12 South's current dominance was "cyclical," 2006

"I don't comment on officiating. I just give out hams is what I do."

*— **Leach**, when asked about the officiating*
after Texas Tech's Gator Bowl victory over Virginia, 2008

"I got fined $10,000 one time for expressing my opinion. I have to leave this one up to you. (But) I saw the same game you did. I think it'd be surprising how close my thoughts are to yours."

*— **Leach**, when asked at a press conference if it*
seemed as though there was an unusual number of calls
subject to interpretation in the Washington State-Nevada game

"You prepare for the games for years, and you remember them the rest of your life. Despite all that, I'm not allowed to comment on the officiating."

— Leach

"As much as I would love to comment on officiating, and I could go on for hours. . . . I'm not interested in paying the price. If I ever do, I'll put on a heck of a press conference. I'll even include audiovisuals."

— Leach

"Rather than coaches and athletic directors being asked about officiating, I think what needs to happen is, after the game, at the press conference, there has to be a representative from the officials answering these questions. Right now, the officials aren't accountable for any of that stuff, and they'll make some screwy call, right, wrong, or indifferent, and there's a coach sitting there, and everybody's asking him. It's a total ambush waiting to happen, because we're not allowed to comment on it. If you do, you get fined. It directly affects the success or failure of your team, whether it's a good call or a bad call. All of a sudden, you're sitting there, and those questions should be directed to the referee, rather than you or the athletic director."

— Leach

"It's a little like breakfast; you eat ham and eggs. As coaches and players, we're like the ham. You see, the chicken's involved, but the pig's committed. We're like the pig; they're like the chicken. They're involved, but everything we have rides on this."

*— Leach, on the officials at the
2007 Texas Tech-Texas game in Austin*

"I never called Dan Beebe in the middle of a game. There was a game that had some questionable calls, and so I did call the head of officials and pointed it out. That's what that was. It wasn't Dan Beebe. I know Dan really well. I talk to Beebe a lot. I talked to him after that one, too."

*— **Leach**, when asked if he called Big 12 commissioner Dan Beebe on his cell phone to complain about the officiating during a game*

"I certainly hope that the good Texas Tech fans will refrain from throwing tortillas for the sake of our football team. Nevertheless, at no level do I see where the Red Raider football team is responsible at all for any tortillas being thrown. We watch over them very carefully, and before they ever go on the field, we ensure that none of them have tortillas.

"If one of our players on the sideline throws a tortilla, it's not going to be a five-yard penalty; I'll kick him off the team. I think that penalties need to be directed at guilty parties instead of innocent parties."

*— **Leach**, after his team was twice penalized for objects being thrown on the field by fans against Missouri*

"I felt like I was talking to his collarbone. But I said, 'Hello, can you hear me? It's Mike Leach here.' The guys in the press box could hear it loud and clear. But my daughter in the stands said, 'Mom, isn't that Dad's voice?' They couldn't understand anything. I guess we could get dogs or post cameras up there to see who's slinging those things."

*— **Leach**, on being asked by referee Steve Usechek to plead with the fans not to throw tortillas. Leach spoke into Usechek's microphone, which was woven into the referee's uniform.*

"It's about as helmet to helmet as you could get. There's a lot of blind people that can tell by hearing that it was helmet to helmet."

> — *Leach, upset that officials did not penalize a Texas player for a hit against Texas Tech quarterback Taylor Potts, 2009*

"For the most part, it wouldn't be stuff that you'd be allowed to print in your paper."

> — *Leach, on what he thought of his team leading the nation in number of penalties and penalty yards per game, to a* Lubbock Avalanche-Journal *reporter*

"That's inexcusable. It's nearly a capital offense based on the level of stupidity that's involved in a false start by a receiver. A receiver's not supposed to listen to the count. He's supposed to be watching the football. The ability to watch a ball and see if it moves, I think that's pretty simple."

> — *Leach*

"I've always thought it was incredibly ridiculous to try to shorten games. People who think the games are too long can turn their TVs off. Or if the game starts at, say, two (o'clock), they can start watching at three. Shortening games is insane."

> — *Leach*

"I think this is such a great idea, they should limit both teams to twenty plays, then it would really get them over quickly. Then everybody go out and tailgate. The players and coaches can mingle with the fans and really share in the whole game-day activity."

— Leach, sarcastically explaining his displeasure at the new NCAA rule designed to speed up games

"Everything on the timeout (proposals) is stupid, and it's not just dumb, it's really dumb. And then everything on changing the clock back to where it used to be is brilliant. That is literally Nobel Prize quality intellect and intelligence going into that."

— Leach

"It's crazy. It's ridiculous. With all due respect to the officials, you've got old guys out there with bifocals trying to identify who lowered their head first."

— Leach, when asked about the NCAA's new rules about tackling, which stipulate that defensive players will be ejected from games for hits that target the head area, 2013

"I'm getting tired of everybody apologizing for playing football. As kids, we were excited to play, even when it wasn't football practice, we'd play football. Now we're nuancing and cluttering this thing up with one thing after another."

— Leach, on the targeting rule and other changes in the game

"It's mystifying to me. It would be a little bit like interpreting the Rosetta Stone."

*— **Leach**, when asked about the NCAA's complicated formula that determines when a team can start pre-season practice*

"For whatever reason, the claim is that whoever is making the decision is backlogged. They have the luxury of putting off the decision, whereas I don't have the luxury of rescheduling games when I'm backlogged. Our games are going to happen when they happen, no matter how long it takes to come to a fair resolution."

*— **Leach**, on anxiously awaiting a ruling from the NCAA regarding the eligibility of a player*

"I really don't know what all the rule changes are for this year, but I'll figure 'em out by halftime of the first game."

*— **Leach***

"It's kind of disturbing if you think about it. With everything that's going on, we're worried about how much air goes into a ball when everybody uses their own ball. It's not like it's a forged football. We waste a lot of time with that, and then we worry about the Kardashians. How can it be that we laugh about England's obsession with the royal family? At least the royal family has college degrees and military service."

*— **Leach**, on why the NFL and its fans should focus their energy and attention on more important issues that the New England Patriots and the deflated football controversy, 2015*

7
That's Entertainment!

"There's not a magic potion. Harry Potter didn't come out here and cast a spell on us. We didn't play good. We were flat."

— **Leach**, after Texas Tech suffered a loss to Oklahoma State, 2005

Mike Leach is an admitted film buff. He can and has played the role of a credible movie critic. He's good friends with Oscar-winning actor Matthew McConaughey and director/producer Peter Berg.

Leach even made a brief, yet memorable cameo appearance on the popular TV series *Friday Night Lights* in 2009.

Many years earlier, while in law school at Pepperdine, Leach dabbled in acting. He had bit roles in two movies, *Grunt! The Wrestling Movie*, in which he played a security guard, and *J. Edgar Hoover*, a TV mini-series in which he portrayed a nonspeaking FBI agent.

During his two years away from coaching in 2010-2011, Leach co-hosted a sports satellite radio show and did color commentary on college games on TV.

He's well-read and has written three books. Leach also likes his music, favoring the likes of such icons as Jimmy Buffett, Neil Young, Lynyrd Skynard, and Jethro Tull.

Howie Stalwick, Kitsap Sun: *What's your favorite movie?*
Leach: "I like all the (director Alfred) Hitchcock stuff. *Rio Bravo* is up there, with John Wayne, Dean Martin, Walter Brennan. Angie Dickinson's in it."

Q: What's your favorite sports movie?
Leach: "It would have to be *Bull Durham*. That first *Rocky* was really good. Baseball and boxing movies are the best sports movies to make because you can stop the action. Football movies are the toughest sports movies to make because you've got twenty-two guys in motion, they're wearing helmets . . . That one football movie, *Friday Night Lights*, they did a tremendous job."

Tom Rinaldi, ESPN: "*What's the most overrated movie of all-time?*"
Leach: *Terms of Endearment* — it's so similar to so many other dialogue movies. . . . Personal preference — it didn't do much for me."

Q: "What's the worst movie ever?"
Leach: "*Vanilla Sky* (starring Tom Cruise) was phenomenally bad."

From Washington State press conference:
Q: "What are your favorite Halloween movies?"
Leach: "The best one ever is *Psycho*. . . . But then you can say that that's not necessarily a monster movie. If you want to stay within that, the best ones, in my opinion, are the first *Halloween* and *The Omen*. There will be some *Exorcist* fans that are ticked off that I don't include that, but that's too bad. It's my list, not theirs."

On Texas Tech running back Harrison Jeffers:
"He's got some Forrest Gump quality to him in what he does there, there's no question. He runs a couple of extra yards. We coach second effort, and we aren't going to do anything to discourage him. He will score and make sure to cover as much of the end zone and a little bit extra."

*— **Leach**, noting that Jeffers, instead of slowing down once he scored, tended to proceed quickly across or through the end zone and hurry back to the sideline*

"I just sort of Forrest Gumped my way into some stuff."

*— **Leach**, on his coaching career*

"*The Goods: Live Hard, Sell Hard* was better than a person would expect, and *Halloween* [one of the sequels] was horrible. . . . I'm not a big science fiction guy, but I think that everybody was surprised that there was finally a good *Star Trek* movie (with Chris Pine now in the lead role as Captain Kirk). It was more like the (TV) series. Sadly, most of those *Star Trek* movies have been worse than an episode of the original series. This *Star Trek*, by far, hands down, no holds barred, is the best *Star Trek* movie that they've had in years. . . . I saw *Inglourious Basterds*, which I thought was decent. I thought that the anticipation was great, didn't think the payoff was as good as you're typically used to in a Quentin Tarantino movie. Even though this was worth seeing, I thought the other ones were better. I thought *Jackie Brown* was better. I thought *Pulp Fiction* was better. Then, of course, the early ones — you know he wrote *True Romance*, which is awesome. And then *Reservoir Dogs*, which is a better movie."

*— **Leach**, offering his summer movie reviews to the media, 2009*

"It's like Sharon Stone said one time after a movie she did, she said, 'No guts, no glory.' And then if we didn't, I felt like we could get it, and we did."

— *Leach, after a fourth-down gamble late in the game worked to help Texas Tech beat Nebraska 37-31 in overtime, 2008*

"Maybe John Cusack. I think we have some similar looks and mannerisms."

— *Leach, when asked what actor should play the role of Mike Leach in his life story*

"What I'd like to have is a guy with a BB gun up there. I don't want any injuries or anything like that, so it'd be a BB gun. And I'd like to have one of those laser pointers like that guy had on *Seinfeld*. Then I'd point to a (player) and they'd give him a quick shot in the butt and (the player) says, 'Oh, did I hesitate? Yeah, I hesitated on that play.' Unless I get a little help from the NCAA, they're probably not going to let me do that."

— *Leach, on his plan to get his players to play with more aggression after playing hesitantly and tentatively during a 70-35 victory over TCU. In that game, Tech faced a 21-0 deficit with 8:06 remaining in the first half before scoring fifty-six unanswered points, 2004*

"First of all, no. But the likelihood of me ever sharing that or anything like that, do you know how many steps there are to the lowest vault in Texas Tech? You have to camp along the way. It's like something out of the *Lord of the Rings*. Unless you know the elves that got the key, and unless you can kill a whole bunch of dwarves to get there, I mean, you'll never get to it. And you have to have the invisible ring anyway to get through the circle of fire, and even Harry Potter can't get it. So the chances of that ever being revealed to anybody in this room is highly unlikely."

— ***Leach***, *when asked if anything was wrong with Texas Tech receiver Detron Lewis, whose playing time had diminished recently*

"Any stuff on that is so closely guarded. I don't know if you saw *Harry Potter*, but in the basement of this building, it's guarded by serpents and wild dogs and things like that, and you can go try to find the secret to that, but chances of survival — always a risk. Heck, it took until movie five before he got it done himself, and he had magic powers. Anyway, he's doing just fine and we're excited about him."

— ***Leach***, *when asked about the health*
of Washington State quarterback Connor Halliday

"I'm sure there is. That's in that same vault guarded by rattlesnakes, rats and a dragon — he's at study hall right now."

— ***Leach***, *when asked if there was a reason why a*
certain Washington State player was missing from practice

"I'm not a big Batman guy, but I do recommend that you go. They have everything from Batman helmets to some cool brass knuckles that the Joker has to Catwoman outfits and some definite villains. You can go upstairs to the Harry Potter exhibit and they'll tell you what tribe you're in, or the fraternity, or whatever. Mine was Huffle-something."

*— **Leach**, on visiting a Batman exhibit at Warner Bros. studio during the Pac-12 Media Day*

"There was a movie with Paul Newman called *The Verdict*. They ask him about the justice system and he says, 'The justice system doesn't give you justice, it gives you a shot at justice.' A shot at it is better than nothing."

*— **Leach**, when asked about the Bowl Championship Series (BCS), 2008*

"As always, suspense, why do people watch games, because of suspense, because they want to know what's going to happen. I'm not a guy that tells people the ending to a movie if they haven't seen it, and I'm certainly not going to share that with you. If you want to know how it turns out, you've got to come see the movie."

*— **Leach**, when asked who would be his starting quarterback in an upcoming game*

"It's kind of like the movie *Patton*. They're getting ready to go in a big battle and they ask Patton, 'How will your guys be?' And he says, 'They'll be fine.' And they said, 'Why do you think they'll be fine?' He says, 'Cause they're trained to be.' Well, we train all the time. I mean, we need to go out there and expect to make plays. We're happy we make plays, but we need to get the mindset where it's a little more expected, where we're not surprised to make plays."

— Leach

"I'm not one of those people that is on the edge of my seat worrying about the draft. I don't think about it. I don't listen to a bunch of dumb prognosticators guess at it. I'm not a person that is sitting there, held in suspense on what is going to happen in the draft. It's a little bit like the Academy Awards. I wait until after it happens and then, maybe, I read it in the newspaper the next day."

— Leach, when asked about his interest in the NFL Draft

"I hope we can get as many as possible out there to the game, and I kind of think we'll get more as time goes on. Everybody will be jacked about getting home on Wednesday with the whole family thing, and then Thursday will hit and they'll eat a whole bunch of turkey. They'll probably watch the parades and see if Underdog is still in the New York parade, even though he's not on TV anymore. Then they'll probably hit a movie sometime Friday. And once they hit Saturday, they'll say, 'Jeez, there is that Tech game,' and we'll have a lot more people than they expect."

— Leach, hoping for a good crowd for a Texas Tech home game against Stephen F. Austin on the Saturday after Thanksgiving

"You'd go there and they'd be watching *M*A*S*H* or something like that, and I'd change the channel to watch *Gunsmoke*. Can you imagine watching *M*A*S*H* or even *Saturday Night Live* when *Gunsmoke's* on? It's almost sacrilegious to anything American, and I tried to get them back on track, which I think I did successfully. Sharon was a bit of a tough case, so I had to marry her where I could keep an eye on her a lot more frequently."

— *Leach, recalling visiting his future wife's apartment in college*

"Yeah, I watch *Desperate Housewives*, and I don't have any apologies. Those women on that show are diabolical, and so are a lot of people I deal with. . . . It's kinda like *Pulp Fiction* with women."

— *Leach*

"Oh, it was real nice. They let me drink Mountain Dew and watch lots of football, so it was pretty good."

— *Leach, describing his experience as a studio guest on a college football highlights show*

"You're going to be dead in a hundred years. Live dangerously."

— *Leach, noting the chance of thunderstorms and advising people to go outdoors anyway, while delivering a weather forecast on a Lubbock TV station*

"I don't think it is an accident that I haven't been asked to do the weather again. I did the best I could at the time, but I will leave it to the professionals. As it stands now, I walk outside in my underwear in the morning and try to gauge it the best I can."

*— **Leach**, when asked by a Washington State fan if he would do a weather forecast on local TV like he once did in Lubbock*

"It was kind of scripted and then it was kind of, 'Well, here's the scenario; do what you want, include this, this, this, and this.' Actually, in the original (filming), there's stuff about Napoleon, Daniel Boone, grizzly bears, raccoons, a bunch of stuff. We covered a lot of bases, and they picked from what they wanted."

*— **Leach**, on his cameo appearance on the* Friday Night Lights *TV show*

"(VIEWERS) JUST GOT A SMALL TASTE OF IT; WE GOT HOURS OF IT. ONE MEETING, THAT'S ALL WE DID WAS TALK ABOUT WAVING THE SWORD ONE WAY OR ANOTHER."

*— **Jamar Wall**, Texas Tech defensive back, on Leach's appearance on* Friday Night Lights

"The things they do good aren't the problem, it's the things they do bad."

*— **Leach**, as a CBS College Sports TV color analyst, describing a 1-8 Memphis team during the broadcast of its game against Tennessee, 2010*

The most points ever scored in a single game by a Mike Leach team (prior to 2016)? In 2005, Texas Tech defeated Sam Houston State, 80-21.

"That's kind of been a constipated effort there by UCF."
> — **Leach**, *as a color analyst during the*
> *North Carolina State-Central Florida telecast, 2010*

"It's a good idea to shave for TV games."
> — **Leach**, *on his game-day appearance as a coach*

"That play was like Shakespeare: much to say about nothing."
> — **Leach**, *commenting on an ill-advised*
> *Tennessee reverse during its game against Memphis, 2010*

"We had too many innocent misunderstandings. We've got a little too much Beaver Cleaver going on out there — 'Well, gee, it's an innocent misunderstanding. It could have happened to anybody.' No, it happens to us all the time. What the hell is that? We've got to get rid of that stuff — this notion that, 'Well, it could have happened to anybody.' No, no, it happened to you, and make sure it doesn't happen to you again. They're not innocent and they're not misunderstandings — they're just lapses in focus and tempo, and that's what we have to get better at."

— *Leach, after Washington State's*
24-20 victory over Eastern Washington, 2012

"I'm not half as alarmed at our demise, like other people are. It's like Mark Twain said: 'The rumors of my death have been greatly exaggerated,' as he appeared alive at that deal. I think our receivers are alive and kicking, despite popular belief."

— *Leach, on replacing his top three receivers at Texas Tech, 2007*

"We're gonna have him do all of it. We're gonna have the defense figure out whether or not they're gonna need to use a linebacker or a safety. It's like Mr. Burns on *The Simpsons*. You know the really mean, greedy rich guy where somebody comes on his property and he says, 'Release the hounds.' And that's kinda what Andrei Lintz is. We're going to release the hounds."

— *Leach, on the versatility of*
Washington State tight end Andrei Lintz

"See, when I was in high school, music was evolving toward disco and that was a very dark time because it was just — it was a horrible, horrible period. To all the disco people out there that I am going to offend, I don't care. I really don't care. If you are a disco person, your music is awful. It's terrible. And the damage it has done to music, we still haven't fully recovered. And, so anyway, as the bottom's melting out of the music world, your choice is to hold your breath toward the future, or you have to go backwards. So a lot of us, we went way back. We're talking Beatles and Buddy Holly, which is obviously way back. And those that held their breath toward the future, well then the overcorrection from music is punk. And then punk came out. And yes, it was an improvement to disco, but I don't think that we're fully happy and fully comfortable with that, and that didn't totally withstand the test of time. But it did usher us into something better."

— *Leach*

"Neil Young, I guess was almost the anti-disco. I've always valued lyrics a great deal. A song should say something instead of just being strictly music, and I always (thought) he had a wide variety of messages. Everything he touched musically, he was a master of. He thought independently when disco personified those who didn't think independently. Neil Young was the ultimate in independent thinking. (He) elevated every group he was ever with. I still like Crosby, Stills, and Nash, but they weren't the same when Neil Young left, not even close. Neil Young's kind of on the list of people I'd most like to meet. I don't imagine he loves meeting people very much, but nevertheless, Neil Young has always been toward the top of my list."

— *Leach*

Tom Rinaldi, *ESPN: "Why has Madonna endured?"*
Leach: "First of all, she commands attention in a lot of areas. . . . I think one of her weakest is actually music, in my opinion."

"They have a lot of tradition there. It's exciting to go there. You know, Tommy Lee (Motley Crue drummer) went there. I don't really have too much of his stuff, but he's a rock 'n' roll icon. So the chance to go play at the school where Tommy Lee was in the band for a very brief period of time's exciting."

— *Leach, on playing at Nebraska, 2005*

"I'm not a huge jump-around guy. I was too self-conscious to dance, really."

— *Leach, talking about not joining the Texas Tech home crowd in celebrating a victory over Oklahoma by dancing to the song* Jump Around

"We may have some kind of a get-together and have a tournament for that. We may have to do that in private, though. Those things aren't typically G-rated."

— *Leach, when asked who the best rapper is on the Washington State team*

8
Meet the Press

"I think what clouds this thing is, and I don't know when it was, probably, about eight years ago, honest answers kind of went out of style. They want you to be honest as long as nobody's feelings get hurt. Well, that's crazy. I mean, I was most critical of myself. We need to quit asking questions if we don't want honest answers."

— **Leach**, on criticism from reporters about publicly criticizing his players after a 49-6 loss to Utah

"Love-hate" might be one way to describe Mike Leach's relationship with the media. Not surprisingly, Leach has his own unique style. He's readily available to reporters via his cell phone; at the same time, he provides considerably less access to his players, preferring they focus on the task at hand.

The coach drew the ire of the Football Writers Association of America, the *Fort Worth Star-Telegram*, and others in 2005 when he selected two players (later expanded to four) to serve as team spokesmen each week. Everyone else was off-limits until after the game.

Leach is usually good for a clever, colorful quote or two. He once interrupted a live radio interview to place his order at a drive-through fast food restaurant.

At press conferences, he usually doesn't make opening statements, but takes questions and sometimes veers off into unusual subjects seemingly unrelated to football. At certain times, like most coaches, he can appear defensive with the media, while having little tolerance for questions he perceives as being "dumb."

His often-calculated remarks seem designed to get either his players' attention/motivate them — see "fat little girlfriends/empty corpses/zombies."

The articulate coach can be brutally frank, funny, and sarcastic at the same time, all the while making a point. Players, officials, administrators — all are subject to his review. What's sometimes forgotten is that Leach will also be critical of himself and his coaching staff. In other words, he doesn't play favorites in a world in which many players expect to be coddled or protected by their coaches.

Perhaps his two most bizarre press conferences occurred immediately following a 49-6 loss to Utah in 2012 and on the ensuing Monday.

In postgame comments, Leach first blamed himself and the coaching staff and then bluntly faulted his team's lack of effort, specifically the offensive and defensive lines. Furthermore, he made the starting linemen come out and face the media to answer questions.

Two days later, at his usual beginning-of-the-week press conference, Leach was questioned about publicly "calling out" his players.

"You do bring up an interesting point because I have considered this over the years, you know, having a 'yes-no' conference where every question is answered with a 'yes' or 'no,'" Leach responded. "And I certainly couldn't rule that out. And if somebody says, 'How did the game go?' I would say, 'OK.' I mean, when we play really well, I say we play really well. I may go to that 'yes-no' thing because, in this era of ridiculous political correctness and stuff like that, there seems to be some dissatisfaction for style points. Typically, if I'm asked a question, I give an honest answer, and I say that there's evidently some dissatisfaction with that."

Leach continued: "But I can go to the one-syllable answer, and I can like that, and it appeals to me. And I've done something a certain way for a number of years, and so maybe it's time to change that and check things out. We'll make this kind and gentle the rest of the way. I'm gonna try it the other way. All right, ask me some questions."

From there, a reporter inquired: "Coach, what do you think this team needs to do in order to make it a successful season?"

To which Leach responded sarcastically: "Well, you know, I think they're doing everything they can to be successful. I think, as a team, we've had a lot of guys participate, and they've had a lot of fun. And they're trying as hard as they possibly can. And everybody wants to win really bad. And they're trying so hard, and I couldn't be any prouder of them. And everybody's done everything we could. And this program this year has taken it as far as we possibly could. And I couldn't be happier with it because we've tried that hard. And I think next year we're gonna be even better because everybody's great and everybody's done a perfect job. And I like the way everything's going."

In the spring of 2015, Leach seemed to adopt this new approach to the media, answering reporters' questions with short, direct, by-the-book responses. His understated, low-key comments were, for the most part, lacking his usual flair or humor.

Abe Lemons, the late college basketball coach, employed a similar "tell it like it is" philosophy during his stints at Oklahoma City University, Pan American, and the University of Texas.

The highly successful coach (599 career wins) was known as much for his sarcastic wit as he was for victories. His biting yet humorous wrath seldom escaped administrators, referees, players, and anyone else in the vicinity.

After he was once criticized for putting down his players publicly, "Honest Abe" offered this Leach-like response:

"I'm not responsible for what other people think. They can take what I say any way they want to. . . . 'Gee-whiz, golly yes, (Johnny) Moore played a great game. He played lovely.' See how my language has changed?"

Lemons went on to offer this insightful comment: "If you win and say that such and such player is slow, everyone laughs. It's funny when you win. If you lose, and you say the same thing, all of a sudden it's criticism. The truth, I guess, is a whole lot funnier when you're winning."

Paul Sorensen, a columnist for Cougfan.com and a former WSU player, went as far as to write this about Leach, following the 3-9 season of 2014:

"When you're winning, a guy who comes across as aloof, stubborn, and short with the media is considered quirky and uniquely endearing. When you're losing, that same guy is considered an ass."

Stefanie Loh, in her first year covering Wazzu and Leach for the *Seattle Times* in 2015, fully appreciated Leach's press conferences: "The man continues to amaze me with his metaphors," she tweeted. "I'll take this, and his sometimes gruff pressers, over plain old Nick Sabanisms any day."

But perhaps the most accurate description of Leach and the media was delivered in a 2008 feature written by David Barron of the *Houston Chronicle*. In that article, Texas Tech student Jared Brannon was quoted as saying that Leach's "interviews never make sense. But they make sense at the same time."

Exactly, Jared.

"I've never been a big opening statement guy. I always find the media asks what they want anyway."

— *Leach, on press conferences*

"Coaches typically spend too much time dealing with criticism. Much of it comes from the media. I think the media are like realtors. My dad, brother, and my sister are realtors. They don't care if the market is up or down; they just want property moving. Action is good for business. That's the way it is with the media, too."

— *Leach*

"I've got half a dozen cowlicks or so I'm told. I try to give the (TV) viewers what they want, which is a sharp, highly decorated-looking figure. Sometimes it requires running your hands through the hair and hoping for the best. It didn't turn out terribly well today."

— *Leach, on fixing his hair shortly before doing a TV interview*

"My players like to say 'vibe' all the time. And I'm down with the youth."

— *Leach, using the word 'vibe' in an answer*

First reporter: *"Just wondering why Brandon Carter was suspended, and what he has to do to get back on the field."*
Leach: "Uh, well, it's not privy to the media. It's for violating team rules, and anything he needs to get back is pretty much between him and me."
Second reporter: *"Can Brandon get back on the team this year? Are there some requirements that he could come back, or is he gone for good?"*

Leach: "Did you listen to [first reporter's] question, and the response to that?"

Second reporter: *"Yeah, but you didn't exactly answer that."*

Leach: "I mean, based on my response to [first reporter's] question, what makes you think you'd get a different one?"

Third reporter: *"For a senior captain to get suspended, how disappointing is that?"*

Leach: "Did you hear my answer to the last question? Well, write that down."

> *— responding to questions about Texas Tech*
> *offensive lineman Brandon Carter at a press conference*

Q: *"Were those kind of uncharacteristic of him; did he maybe have a little too much confidence in his arm or something?"*

Leach: "Did you see the game?"

> *— **Leach** not happy with a postgame question regarding*
> *the four interceptions thrown by quarterback Luke Falk*

Q. *"Is there ever a concern when sending in a player that hasn't been playing for most of the game that they might be cold or might not be able to jump in and be warm right in the game?"*

Leach: "Next question. I mean, what the hell kind of question is that? You go out there, you practice all the time, you play. I'm not even answering that. Next one."

Q. *"A couple times this season when things go wrong, they go wrong quickly and drastically. Why is that? How can that be fixed?"*

Leach: "Next question."

> *— New Mexico Bowl postgame press conference, after Washington*
> *State yielded a sizable lead and lost to Colorado State, 2013*

"Are you an idiot or something? I mean, seriously. Next question."

> — *Leach, when asked by a reporter after a loss to Stanford if he should have protected a late lead by running instead of passing*

"Anybody would have run their offense and tried to score in that situation. Unless you want me to provide you some of that same education I did that last guy, why don't you go ahead and leave the strategy to me and we'll leave writing the articles to you."

> — *Leach, again being questioned about throwing the ball instead of running while protecting a lead*

"We have to straighten out the kicking. Do you really feel like that's a good question? They already have hurt us. We've missed six extra points. It's cost us six points. You think I have a crystal ball? Next question."

> — *Leach, tired of being questioned about the Red Raiders' woes in the kicking game, 2008*

"There's more computers and ballpoint pens and TV stations at a lot of other places than at Lubbock."

> — *Leach, on why Texas Tech football doesn't receive more national recognition*

"AT KICKOFF, I PRAY THAT THE LORD WILL GIVE HIM (SON ADAM) THE FOCUS THAT HE NEEDS TO DO HIS JOB AND FOR ME TO DO MY JOB. I LOOK AT IT IF I DON'T CALL THE GAME HONEST, I WON'T GO BACK AND DO ANOTHER ONE OF HIS GAMES. EVERYBODY WHO HAS LISTENED TO THOSE GAMES WAS AMAZED THAT I COULD DO IT. I DID IT TOTALLY UNBIASED. IF (TEXAS TECH COACH) MIKE LEACH MESSES UP, I'M GOING TO SAY SOMETHING ABOUT IT. IF THEY ARE NOT GOING TO DO THEIR JOB, I POINTED IT OUT."

— *Craig James, ESPN broadcaster, asked if he was objective in broadcasting Texas Tech games in which his son Adam was on the team, November 13, 2009*

Q: *"Could the loss to TCU be beneficial based on what the team learned from that experience?"*

Leach: "I hope so. Everybody talks about how beneficial losses are. If they were so beneficial, everybody would lose twelve times and be real smart. I mean, whatever gets you through the night, it's nice of you to say. Maybe that's the case, so we'll go with that, because that's about all we have. We don't get to play them again."

"I think their head's in the newspaper. I think those guys are reading too many press clippings, buying into everyone saying how good they are. They haven't played a down yet this year. They haven't proven a thing. We don't know that we can beat Lubbock High School right now."

— *Leach, displeased with Texas Tech's veteran players during spring workouts*

"Here's the thing — and, of course don't get me wrong, this isn't a rip on the media. But I freely rip on the media, as you guys well know, if I feel like it. But certainly the important thing about media is it generates all kinds of attention, support, makes it exciting for a broader faction of people than just players and coaches. So I think it's a critical role and a very important role and fun and exciting role for everybody.

"But I'll tell you if you're a football team, and a guy eighteen to twenty years old trying to reach your maximum potential, and you don't have the discipline to keep your nose out of the newspaper and have one eye looking — and as coaches, too — how good you are, and this and that, it's just, it makes your efforts toxic, and it's unfortunate we didn't have the discipline to do that, that's the part that's most disappointing."

*— **Leach**, after Texas Tech's upset loss to Texas A&M, 2009*

"I thought over those two weeks we got soft and passive and we got complimented too many times over the Nebraska game. We were more concerned with doing interviews than having practice. After that game, I decided that we would adjust that a little bit. It got to be a distraction. Guys were thinking the most important part of their job was giving interviews rather than making plays. I just wanted to see how they would play."

*— **Leach**, on his controversial policy limiting media access to two players. His decision came after Texas Tech's 70-10 victory over Nebraska, followed by a 51-21 loss to Texas, 2004*

"Our young people have the opportunity to divorce themselves from the distractions and try to stay focused on the game ahead. Second, and probably most important, is the fact that these are eighteen- and nineteen-year-old young guys who don't have necessarily a great deal of experience with some of the dialogue that takes place with the media."

> — *Leach, explaining his limited-access media policy. Following games, most Texas Tech players were available for media interviews — but during Tech's weekly Monday press conference, only two Red Raiders — quarterback Cody Hodges and cornerback Khalid Naziruddin — were made available. No further access was allowed until after the game, 2005*

"IF LEACH THINKS THAT HODGES AND NAZIRUDDIN SHOULD BE THE SOLE CHRONICLERS OF THE TEXAS TECH SEASON, HE'S GUILTY OF TRYING TO ORCHESTRATE WHAT GOES INTO OUR NEWSPAPER. SO WE'LL MAKE IT EASY FOR THE HEAD COACH. WE'LL SEE HIM ONLY ON SATURDAYS (GAME DAYS)."

> — *Gil LeBreton, Fort Worth Star-Telegram, on the newspaper's decision to provide no coverage beyond Tech game stories*

"What they may say has never been one of my fears. It's just so that they avoid distractions of their own. We had a process where we had too many guys aspiring to be team spokesmen."

> — *Leach, on limiting the availability of players to the media*

"So much before games, players spend all their time talking about what they're going to do. Some of it they get drawn into, because, obviously, if you're writing a story before a game, from a media standpoint, there's major speculation on what's going to happen, how it's going to be, creating a level of anticipation, things like that.

"But from a player's standpoint, that's not always a healthy deal to have some young guy that's still kind of learning his role on the team to sit and tell you all the stuff he's going to do. In some cases, they make poor, sloppy comments, but in some cases, just that opportunity gets them distracted and gets their head a little fuller than it should be."

*— **Leach**, on why he limited media access to a few Texas Tech players during the week of games*

"I just don't like it when players talk about what they're going to do. How do they know what they're going to do? I don't even know what they're going to do. I know what I'd like them to do. I know that's funny stuff to talk about, but it doesn't have anything to do with the game, and it's a distraction. I just want to minimize the distractions. I don't think that's so wrong."

*— **Leach***

"On a certain level, after a pretty good game, I think it's a bit of a privilege to speak to the media. (It's) some level of recognition — even if the results were disappointing, just the fact that your opinion counts for something. We weren't entitled to that, not the way we played, not on special teams or offense. That, and I wanted them to think about how we played. I wanted them to think about what our performance was, not to just waltz out there and spin doctor what it was and find a bunch of positives, because there isn't a bunch of positives. There's no alibis for not playing hard every play. There's none."

— *Leach, on not allowing the Texas Tech offensive and special team units to talk to the media after a 37-13 loss to Colorado, 2002*

"He is just a shy person and devotes his time to thinking about football. Just the ability to be that focused that quickly at that young of an age has always impressed me. In my view, his priorities were catching footballs instead of doing high-falutin' interviews. So I like that, too. With all due respect to you guys. And I if ever hear him saying something, I will be happy to tell you because he is a little hard to track down."

— *Leach, on Texas Tech star receiver Michael Crabtree and his reluctance to be in the media spotlight*

"We're not mentally tough enough to respond to the media or to read the newspapers without losing track of what our job is."

*— **Leach**, on not allowing media access to Texas Tech players after a 51-21 loss to Texas*

"I don't think it hurts to have them take ownership in the team. It's interesting to me, which I don't care. I get media all the time saying, 'Can I talk to somebody, can I talk to somebody, can I talk to somebody?' Well, conservatively speaking, I gave them twenty people to talk to, but they didn't like the ones I selected to talk to. Then, of course, they complained. Not most, but a few. If O-linemen and D-linemen aren't a guy's cup of tea, that's too bad, you don't have to ask them any questions. I think they're valuable members of our team, and I think they're certainly guys that take ownership in our team, and there's certainly some players there that I'm very proud of, and, well, anybody that doesn't like offensive linemen and defensive linemen really aren't my type of people. I coached offensive line for ten years. So if you don't like offensive linemen, I'll be nice to you, I'll be polite, but you're really not my kind of guy."

*— **Leach**, on criticism that he forced his linemen to face the media after a poor effort in Washington State's 49-6 loss to Utah*

"I've been criticized for not doing what 'big-time' programs do, so I've decided to accommodate the wishes of the media. And 'big-time' programs like to have game-time decisions, so we've got us a game-time decision on our hands, and I think that'll be not just 'big-time' for everyone, but exciting for everyone. So there's 'big-time' for you, how do you like that?"

*— **Leach**, on keeping the media guessing as to who would be his starting quarterback, 2009*

"We're going to treat the next three games all dramatically differently, and then there will be all kinds of interesting little twists and nuances that we'll do to each individual one to dignify it for its importance that exists in the overall scheme of the universe. There'll be dramatic differences, and, throughout the course of the deal, I'll enjoy talking about it in length."

— Leach, on the importance of three upcoming road games in a row, 2002

Leach, during a postgame news conference after a loss to Oklahoma, noticing reporters feverishly writing in their notebooks:

"They're a good team. Like I say, anytime you play somebody good, the margin of error is narrowed. God, there's a lot of left-handed people in here. (Laughter) I'm left-handed, you know. Well, I throw right-handed, just for the record. How about that?

"(To a reporter) Are you left-handed? You are? No way. Are you kidding me? Everybody raise their hands. Let's see who's left-handed. We're about 50 percent in here. "

Q: *"Do you find left-handed people to be more creative?"*

Leach: "I don't know. They say that. I think it's sort of by process of elimination, and half the room knows what I'm talking about here. If you spent your time in high school and grade school with the three-ring, loose-leaf binder, which is a complete curse, you know something's got to be going your way. It finally got to where I turned it upside down . . . so I'd never have to run over the thing. But it really was a nightmare.

"Scissors are interesting, too. That's a developed skill. . . .

"There's two types of journalists — there's a guy that wants to write the Great American Novel; then there's the type that wants to do a good, solid job, have some creativity; then there's the type that are just slackers. They're the ones really into injuries. The reason is they're not creative enough to keep their stories interesting. They're not ambitious enough."

— Leach

"I wish I had something really flashy for you guys you could do exposés on and win Nobel Prizes and all the rest. But the thing about it is, you've got to do the same thing over and over again and do (it) better."

— Leach, at a press conference, on the importance of a team's fundamentals

"I know I'm talking to a group of (media) people that love to draw all kinds of conclusions. 'This means this, and that means that. If a guy went around the stadium with a hot dog, what would happen next?' But the truth of the matter is, this conference has been decided in the last week or the last two weeks for a long, long time. This season's going to go twelve games, and we need to play all twelve games to the end."

— Leach, emphasizing there was no reason for his team to panic after a conference loss, 2003

"I try to be polite and answer it, but it's very difficult to kind of not roll your eyes at the thing. There's nothing wrong with the scheme. How it's applied, how you play, how hard you try, yeah, that's infested with problems right now."

— Leach, when asked if opponents had learned how to stop the Tech offense, 2006

"If your opinion really mattered to me, you'd probably be invited to some of the staff meetings around here. And unless that invitation's gotten lost in the mail, I don't guess you were."

         — *Leach, responding bluntly to a radio interviewer who questioned the team's unity under Leach at Washington State, 2012*

"He's thrown a higher percentage than any quarterback we've had. (To waitress) Yeah, I'm No. 7. (pause) . . . Last year, he was kind of a, well, he was a sophomore."

     — *Leach, during a Big 12 teleconference, interrupting his thoughts on quarterback Kliff Kingsbury, to place an order at Chicken Express, 2001*

"We're watching film here. One time I got in trouble for ordering lunch on one of these deals, so I'll probably read about watching film here and letting that interrupt this press conference. I ordered Chicken Express one time and that wasn't a big hit. . . . Uh, yeah, anyway, go ahead."

     — *Leach, during a Big 12 media teleconference. After answering a question, Leach was overheard saying something to someone in the room with him. He then cut off the moderator to explain what was distracting him.*

"I hope the next Graham Harrell or Michael Crabtree are sitting in their living room and they are astute, studious guys in addition to being talented. They say, 'I know what, the NFL game is over but I want to watch *60 Minutes*. Oh, Texas Tech on *60 Minutes*.' That's me, and then they come here. Hopefully, it will turn out that way."

     — *Leach, on being profiled on CBS-TV's* 60 Minutes, *2009*

"I think Twitter is stupid to begin with. I'm not going to sit around with a bunch of narcissists that want to sit around and type stuff about themselves. We'll put mirrors in some of their lockers, if that's necessary, but they don't have to twitter."

— *Leach, on banning his players from using Twitter at Texas Tech*

"When football was invented, the sanctuary for players was the locker room. Guys could go in the locker room and relax and talk among their teammates. It's not for public consumption. They don't need to be in a position where they're worrying about a coach or a player tweeting what they said or what they did or how their practice went or what plays will be run or how much they're going to play that week. . . . A lot of that was sacred information before Twitter, and it's still sacred. It doesn't need to be shared on the outside because it disintegrates the team effort, to where the team is essentially playing against itself. If it gets out of hand, the biggest adversary is not your opponent that week; the biggest adversary is trust and a bad team setting."

— *Leach*

"If someone has a quilting bee and sensitive material is discussed, or personal information is discussed, you don't gossip about it on the outside to everybody else, or you're not going to be invited back to make quilts. I don't think any of that has really changed."

— Leach

"Twitter is now banned around here, so don't expect anything on Twitter.... Twitter's banned, and, quite frankly, if after today you see anything on Twitter from our team — and I don't care if it says, 'I love life' — I would like to see it because I will suspend them."

— Leach, in his first season at Washington State

"These are high-profile players at USC, for goodness sakes. They have their Twitter handle next to their name on their two-deep roster."

— Leach, after Washington State upset USC, 10-7, 2013

9
Sideline Pass
(Halftime Interviews)

"Why would you ask a dumb question like that?"

— **Lloyd Carr**, Michigan coach, to a halftime interviewer

Most serious college football fans cringe when they see the intrepid sideline TV reporter approaching an intense coach on the field for a quick halftime interview. Let's be honest. In the heat of battle, what reasonably intelligent question can one ask and what reasonably intelligent answer can one provide?

Perhaps the most famous exchange occurred in 2003. Allow us to set the scene:

With less than a minute remaining in the first half of its annual showdown with Ohio State, Michigan had the ball on its own thirty-yard line, holding a 21-7 lead. Despite the fact that the Wolverines had two timeouts remaining, Coach Lloyd Carr decided to run out the clock. As they headed into the tunnel, ABC's Todd Harris had the following exchange with Carr:

Harris: "Well, Coach, I know you get second-guessed all week long, but how come you didn't go with anything when you have two timeouts left in the half?"

Carr: "Why would you ask a dumb question like that?"

Harris: "Well, I'm just curious with forty-four seconds left with a

116

chance to make a move down the field and possibly get a field goal."

Carr: (stares for a second then walks away, appearing to smile and shake his head)

Harris: "All right, Keith (Jackson), back to you. I guess Coach didn't want to answer that."

Michigan ended up winning, 35-21, and Carr later apologized to the interviewer.

Perhaps the "best" halftime interview was University of Texas coach Mack Brown, who retired after the 2013 season. The unflappable, personable Brown could take a basic question and turn it into a prolonged "I'm in your living room" recruiting monologue.

Brown expounded on this in a 2014 interview with *The Oklahoman*:

"People talk about coaches having coachspeak and they'll never tell you the truth and they won't talk to you. The truth is, every time a coach is speaking, he's speaking to the parents of his players, or he's speaking to the high school coaches, or he's speaking to the mother and dad of a recruit. It's all about recruiting. Nothing else."

And then there's the Mike Leach approach.

He readily admits that he hates halftime interviews, and, in fact, jogs to the dressing room, forcing the reporter to chase him for a quick word. When cornered, Leach, with a look on his face that seems to say he'd rather face a firing squad, usually offers a simple but direct response and then trots away. Still, all in all, it makes for entertaining television.

"My suggestion is, don't wear high heels. Sometimes, they'll (female sideline reporters) go too fashionable. I've had some fun over the years making them run a little bit and watching those high heels sink into the ground."

— *Leach, offering interviewing tips*

"Well, there really isn't a good question. Keep the question kind of open and let the coach talk. Occasionally, they'll ask something specific, which is just mind-numbingly dumb. As a coach, you're kind of impatient at that point, anyway. He knows that you basically want him to talk, and he rattles off whatever he wants to rattle off. Typically, it's not very good. In my case, I don't know if it ever was. . . . I can't even remember one question I've ever been asked. I know my comments are just to make them go away, and I'm certainly not alone in that."

— *Leach, offering more advice to sideline reporters*

Adrian Karsten, *ESPN:* "*Coach, do you feel like the momentum is coming back to your side of the field?*"
Leach: "I don't know — we're not playing worth a damn, and we need to play better than we are right now."

— *With Texas Tech trailing Iowa, 10-3, at the half at the 2001 Alamo Bowl. Iowa won, 19-16.*

Emily Jones, *Fox Sports: "Uh, Mike, great way to start and end the half, but in the middle not so much."*

Leach: "Yeah, in-between not worth a damn. Lookin' forward to the second half."

Jones: *"How's Taylor?"*
Leach: "I don't know."

> — *spoken with Texas Tech leading New Mexico, 14-7, at the half, and starting quarterback Taylor Potts out injured. Tech went on to win, 48-28, 2009.*

Shelley Smith, *ESPN: "How are you stopping Oregon's run?"*
Leach: "By making routine plays."
Smith: *"How do you do that in the second half?*
Leach: "Keep doing it. By making routine plays."

> — *spoken with Washington State trailing second-ranked Oregon, 23-19, at the half. Oregon won, 51-26, 2012.*

Samantha Steele, *ESPN: "Coach, you told me before the game that this game would show you areas that you needed to work on. What will be your focus in the second half?"*

Leach: "Well, we're trying to make too much happen, we just got to relax. We're trying to do too much. We're playing frantic."
Steele: *"Tell me what you think about (quarterback) Jeff Tuel's performance so far this evening."*
Leach: "Ah, average."

> — *spoken with Washington State trailing BYU at the half, 24-6. BYU won, 30-6. 2012*

"Offensively, we squandered the whole first half. Defensively, we played good. Now, we need to play a complete half. . . . He's 100 percent healthy and can run about as fast as he usually can, which is 4.9."
— *Leach, halftime interview with his team leading eighth-ranked Stanford at the half and on the health of his quarterback Luke Falk*

Leach: "I didn't know he had thrown so many times. I guess we'll have to watch out for that in the second half. Have a happy halftime."
— *To sideline reporter Emily Jones at halftime of the 2006 Baylor game. He was responding to the fact that Texas Tech quarterback Graham Harrell had thrown forty-three passes in the first half, in which Tech led, 28-14. Harrell finished 35-of-52 with four touchdown passes in a 55-21 victory.*

"Stop playing fat and lazy."
— *Leach, when asked what his team needed to do in the second half*

Jemele Hill, ESPN sideline reporter, when asked who her favorite interview subject was:

"(WASHINGTON STATE COACH) MIKE LEACH. YOU KNOW GOING INTO IT THAT HE LOVES TO ANTAGONIZE REPORTERS. I LIKE THAT. I DID A PREGAME INTERVIEW WITH HIM WHEN WASHINGTON STATE PLAYED AT UNLV, AND EVEN THOUGH WE WERE MOMENTS FROM KICKOFF, HE REFUSED TO TELL ME WHO WAS STARTING AT QUARTERBACK. AND, HE'S ALSO A 'WALKER,' MEANING HE WALKS AS YOU INTERVIEW HIM. I'M JUST GLAD I DIDN'T TRIP OVER ANYTHING."

10
Politics, Religion, Dating, and Marriage

"Well, I think the results were about what everybody expected. I share the same opinion that 97 percent of the others do."

— **Leach**, on Craig James losing his U.S. Senate bid in Texas

Craig James, the nemesis of Mike Leach during the coach's abrupt termination at Texas Tech, had a less-than-successful run for the U.S. Senate in Texas. The former ESPN college football announcer received just 3.6 percent of the vote in the 2012 Republican primary.

James was one of nine candidates on the ballot, with Texas Lt. Gov. David Dewhurst and former Solicitor Ted Cruz placing first and second respectively. Cruz went on to win in an upset in the runoff and then defeated Democratic nominee Paul Sadler in November. (Four years later, Cruz would run for president.)

James, a former SMU and NFL running back, left ESPN after the 2011 college football season to enter politics. He later joined Fox Sports, but was soon let go from that job.

The outcome of the election should not have come as a surprise to James. During the campaign, in a statewide poll conducted by Lincoln Park Strategies, it was revealed that James was less popular in West Texas than President Obama.

Also, in March of 2012, a *Dallas Morning News* online poll asked readers, "Between Mike Leach and Craig James, who gets your vote?"

Leach received 95.86 percent of the votes, compared to James's 4.14 percent.

"SOMETIMES KIDS GET SO USED TO COACHES WHO ARE POLITICAL, AND WHEN YOU RUN INTO SOMEONE LIKE MIKE WHO'S GOING TO BE BRUTALLY HONEST, IT DOESN'T SIT WELL WITH 'EM. IF YOU CAN'T PLAY, HE'S GOING TO TELL 'EM HE CAN'T PLAY. HE DOES THINGS HIS OWN WAY AND HE'S BEEN SUCCESSFUL. HE'S NOT INTO AP-PEASEMENT."

— *Hal Mumme*, *McMurry coach, who hired Leach as offensive line coach at Iowa Wesleyan in 1989 and took Leach with him to Valdosta State and Kentucky as his offensive coordinator*

"I have never run for office, not even student council. We don't say, 'Hey, you 125 guys, how do you want to practice today?' This isn't a democracy."

— *Leach*, *on coaching authority*

"My favorite is (Sandra Day) O'Connor. I don't believe she lets her political beliefs get in the way of her common sense, which a lot of times I think is a temptation."

— *Leach*, *when asked who his favorite Supreme Court Justice was*

"I like a playoff system. But as for Congress, I think it's really irre-sponsible for the government to waste taxpayer dollars on something like this, especially when there's so much else going on. That takes a lot of audacity, and I think there are other things Congress should concern itself with."

— *Leach*, *on Congress getting involved in the controversy surrounding a college football playoff, 2009*

"I also think this notion of political correctness contaminates it. The First Amendment is . . . everyone should have free speech. It doesn't say you should have free speech unless it hurts someone's feelings. It didn't say that."

— *Leach, speaking to a gathering of Republican women in Lubbock*

"Just watching the election (campaign coverage), I hear all these people that like Donald Trump or hate Donald Trump — well, why does he have so much momentum? Because he's doing what everybody else wants to do, wants to get back to, which is speak honestly."

— *Leach, on the outspoken Republican presidential candidate, 2015*

"That's why you have practice. It's like churches. You have churches for people that sin. You have practice for people that aren't perfect players."

— *Leach, on a freshman's inconsistent performance in practice*

"Basically, I'm a religious person, but with some clear obedience and discipline issues."

— *Leach*

"We had a little revival, I guess. So most of them said, 'Hallelujah.' And that was it."

— *Leach, when asked what he did in a Sunday meeting to impress upon some of his Texas Tech players that they didn't give good effort the day before against Oklahoma State*

"We (didn't just get) our feet wet last year, we got baptized."
— *Leach, reflecting on his first season at*
Washington State, when the team went 3-9

"It seems like everybody kissed and made up. If you get 130 priests together, there's going to be some battles."
— *Leach, on a post-practice fight between*
two back-up players during two-a-days

"This is a big step for Texas Tech. Moses was in high school the last time these people lost a homecoming game. I've talked about the crowd and the stadium and the tradition and the ghosts that circle around here. It's a great team win. Hanging in there as an entire team was the best part."
— *Leach, after defeating Nebraska, 34-31,*
on a last-second touchdown, 2005

"I've always been fascinated by somebody that's an atheist that does believe in ghosts. How can you be an atheist and believe in ghosts?"
— *Leach*

"Really, what we're talking about here is bad manners. Should you be allowed to do this, that, and the other thing? With all this politically correct crap that we've got going on in this country, we're trying to figure out where a line is so everybody is allowed to be ridiculously touchy about everything.

"This (name-calling) has been going on since the playground. I learned about name-calling when I was in kindergarten. Words are just words, and that's always been the case. Then somebody says, 'They hurt my feelings.' Well, too bad. Be tougher than that and have self-esteem that's not going to allow you to get your feelings hurt."

— *Leach, on Oklahoma State basketball player Marcus Smart reacting aggressively to being verbally attacked by a Texas Tech fan, 2013*

"There's very little salad at Cagle's (steakhouse), so the girl will be forced to eat in front of you, which is something that women hate. But if you can make them do it, the earlier the better, the more they'll conversate and show their true self. I'm a big movie guy. If you want to do more like I did when I was your age, you can go to the Stars and Stripes drive-in theater because that's what they had in Cody, Wyoming. But then you want to end it somewhere like some cool coffee shop type of place, where there's bizarre-looking characters going in and out. So if the conversation isn't going well, you can reference some of the characters you see coming and going from the place. And then, if it's a huge night and you're really having a good time, then you can trade computer schemes. And emails and all that mischief people are up to nowadays, which I know nothing about."

— *Leach, offering dating advice to a college freshman in Lubbock*

"One thing that's very important — certainly if you're a guy — you need to go somewhere you can talk. Like this business where there's going to be incessant noise or if you go to some kind of dance club where there's not even guitar music but something that's made by a machine — which is awful and they need to outlaw it — Europe's embraced it for years, and since Europe's supposed to be more sophisticated than us, I don't see it going away anytime soon. The other thing with regard to the girl you take out is to make sure she eats. If they'll eat in front of you, then you know that you're making good progress and that you'll have a chance of good dialogue and a good relationship. Try to make pretty girls eat in front of you and then you're making progress, I would think. . . . How, ultimately, are you really going to be really very good friends with anybody who won't eat in front of you?"

*— **Leach**, offering more dating advice*

"Went to A&W (root beer stand), had just finished a rugby game, went to A&W, had a coupon book. She said, 'What are you getting?' She's looking at the menu. 'What looks good? What are you getting?' I handed her the two-for-one coupon book. I said, 'I don't know, but here's the menu.' Seems to me we got some kind of bacon hamburger thing. She got a root beer freeze. I do remember that. . . . It's worked out pretty good, because I've been married . . . I can't remember, a long time. Thirty years or something."

*— **Leach**, when asked about his first date with his wife*

"Girlfriends are difficult enough without being fictitious. Computers definitely have a big brother quality, which is kinda eerie."

*— **Leach**, on Notre Dame player Manti Te'o's mysterious girlfriend*

"HE GAVE US A SWORD . . . WITH A BIG CARD THAT SAYS, 'FOR THE COUPLE THAT HAS EVERYTHING: SWING YOUR SWORD.'. . . "I THINK SHE (HIS WIFE) LIKES THE SWORD."

— *Matthew McConaughey, actor and newlywed, telling* Tonight Show *host Jay Leno about his wedding gift from friend Mike Leach*

"I didn't think anybody else would get him a pirate sword. Because if you get him a blender, a kitchen clock, or a set of plates or some silverware, you run the risk of being the fifth person that got him that. So I felt like I could monopolize the pirate sword category."

— *Leach, on why he gave McConaughey a sword as a wedding gift*

"There's a part in weddings where all the women are racing around changing their position on virtually every subject. Their moods go up and down, and they are never in the middle. You just try to disappear until it's over, and then you shake everybody's hand and pat them on the back . . . It was a quick, practical, worry-free deal. Like me, she wanted a small wedding, and that worked out well because the payouts and presents doesn't equal the aggravation."

— *Leach, on his daughter's wedding*

". . . It (planning the logistics of the bowl trip) was done in five days. One of the smartest decisions I made is, we were engaged for just two weeks. If you're engaged for a year or two years, that's how long you drag out the hectic nature of things. I didn't realize what a stroke of genius (the short two-week engagement) was until it was over. If I had it to do over again, it (the engagement) would be three days. Of course, we weren't worried about getting more practices in or anything like that."

— *Leach, comparing the benefits of Washington State playing in the first bowl game of the post-season to his wedding engagement*

"We've never really been big on anniversary gifts. I think one time, I took her to a Neil Young concert — she was pretty fired up about that. We always go kinda simple (dinner and a movie) because if you plan too much, you put too much pressure on each other, then it wrecks the whole experience, and by the end of the night, you're wishing you weren't married."

— *Leach, offering advice on celebrating wedding anniversaries*

"Let your wife give you all the names she likes, but retain veto power. She'll fire 150 to you from my experience. Just have the power to veto. Just know you'll have to be satisfied with somewhere in the neighborhood of ten of them. Of the 150, there will be ten acceptable names. Try to avoid the locale names, too. In Texas, I get a kick out of this, every kid will be named Dallas, Austin, or Houston. Now why would a kid want that? About one-third of his class already has it. I would avoid that. Try and avoid the trends, but, by all means, retain veto power. That way, your kid has a fighting chance to hang out with the cool kids. Sometimes, people try too hard. Everybody can name their kid whatever they want. Our (Washington State) best wide receiver is River (Cracraft). I couldn't be happier with that."

— *Leach, when asked what advice he would give a father in naming his son*

11
Pirates and
Other Adventures

"The players really got into the whole pirate thing. We were the 'Pirate Team.' I'll never forget that day Coach Leach came into the meeting with that sword and started explaining how pirates lived. It was wild, but it made so much sense as he got into it. We took three things from that speech: Don't hesitate. Be smart. And be violent on the field. We were a young team and that pirate thing gave us an identity. We needed an attention-getter. We needed something to rally behind. That was it.

"Whenever people find out I played at Texas Tech, they ask how the pirate thing came about. When I explain it, they go, 'You know, that actually makes a lot of sense.' But I know they think it sounds crazy at first."

— **Antonio Huffman**, Texas Tech cornerback (2003-05)

In December 2005, the world *really* discovered Lubbock and Texas Tech, along with Mike Leach and his fascination with pirates. This happened, in great part, thanks to an in-depth profile ("Coach Leach Goes Deep, Very Deep") by Michael Lewis in the *New York Times Magazine*.

Lewis's lengthy piece cited an instance when Leach, after a tough loss, marched the team into the conference room on Sunday morning. For the next three hours, he delivered a lecture on the history of pirates. Leach read from his favorite pirate history, *Under the Black Flag*, by David Cordingly, and used the pirates as an analogy to football.

Before you could say "Blackbeard," Leach's mailbox was being bombarded with pirate artifacts and memorabilia from fans around the country. Tech basketball coach Pat Knight even got into the act, giving Leach a standup pirate dummy with an automated recording to eerily greet visitors to his office.

Tech fans quickly jumped on board, wearing pirate clothing and displaying pirate flags at games.

Suddenly, the winning team, its coach, students, and fans had a full-fledged national identity.

While he was at Texas Tech, Mike Leach's Red Raiders won seven of ten games against rival Texas A&M.

"Based on what people get tagged with in sports, I'm thankful each day that my tag is with pirates rather than with others. You can do a lot worse than pirates."

— Leach

"WE FLEW INTO ORLANDO AND DROVE TO KEY WEST TO RECRUIT THIS KICKER AND LISTENED TO JIMMY BUFFETT THE WHOLE WAY. BUFFETT WAS ALWAYS SINGING ABOUT PIRATES; THAT'S WHERE THE PIRATE THING COMES FROM."

— Hal Mumme, recalling a recruiting trip when he was head coach at Iowa Wesleyan and Leach was an assistant on the staff

"HE GOT HIS POINT ACROSS BETTER THAN ANYONE I'VE EVER SEEN. SOMETIMES IN TEAM MEETINGS, WE'RE TALKING ABOUT A FOOTBALL PLAY, THEN THE NEXT THING YOU KNOW, HE'S TALKING ABOUT PIRATES AND SWORDS OR A DOG PEEING ON HIS TENT WHEN HE WAS A LITTLE KID. PEOPLE WOULD BE LOOKING AROUND LIKE, 'WHERE'S HE GOING WITH THIS ONE?'"

— Eric Morris, former Texas Tech receiver

"HE'S BEEN TALKING ABOUT PIRATES SINCE MY FRESHMAN YEAR. HE DOES IT IN TEAM MEETINGS. HE'LL WALK IN WITH THE SWORD, AND EVERYBODY WILL THINK, 'OH, MAN, HERE WE GO.' AND HE'LL GO ON WITH THE PIRATE STORY. HE LOVES PIRATES."

— Vincent Meeks, Texas Tech safety, 2005

"WE USED TO GO TO THE MOVIES ON FRIDAY NIGHTS BEFORE A GAME AND THEN WE WOULD COME BACK AS A TEAM, AND HE WOULD GIVE HIS FINAL TALK AND GAME-PLANNING SESSION. BEFORE THE 2003 TEXAS GAME, WE WATCHED *MASTER AND COMMANDER* AND HE GETS OUT A WHITEBOARD AND STARTS DRAWING THIS WAR WITH ALL THESE BATTLESHIPS AND HOW THE PIRATES CAME IN AND PROTECTED IT. WE WERE THERE LISTENING TO HIM ABOUT IT FOR MAYBE TWO HOURS AND HE JUST ALWAYS HAD THE BIGGEST KICK, SHARING STORIES ABOUT WHAT PIRATES DID. EVERYONE KNOWS HIS HISTORY AND LOVE OF PIRATES. THAT'S WHERE THE WHOLE 'SWING YOUR SWORD' KIND OF ALL DEVELOPED. HE ALWAYS WOULD SAY, 'WHENEVER YOU'RE TRAPPED AND YOU HAVE NOWHERE TO GO, YOU JUST 'SWING YOUR SWORD!'"

— ***Josh Rangel***, *former Texas Tech safety*

"Pirates function as a team. There were a lot of castes and classes in England at the time. But with pirates, it didn't matter if you were black, white, rich, or poor. The object was to get a treasure. If the captain did a bad job, you could just overthrow him."

— ***Leach***

"The most exciting is Blackbeard. Perhaps my favorite with regards to efficiency and execution would be Bartholomew Roberts. Don't forget about Sir Francis Drake, though. Henry Morgan is interesting, but he betrayed his men."

— ***Leach***, *giving his assessment of several famous pirates/seamen*

Howie Stalwick, Kitsap Sun: *"If you could sit down for dinner or a drink with one person in history, who would it be?"*

Leach: "Geronimo. You talk about a guy ridiculously competitive, ridiculously passionate. One of the ultimate overachievers."

Leach, at a weekly press conference, on why he's fascinated by Geronimo. He and co-author Buddy Levy wrote a book on Geronimo in 2014:
"Geronimo, I always liked, when I was a kid, which was before most of you were kids. They used to have open backyards and dogs used to run all over the neighborhood and so did kids. Now, a lot of times it seems like folks don't know their neighbors, but you'd have a herd of kids running all over, and, of course, back then, you'd play cowboys and Indians. And, of course, the greatest television show of all time — you know, there's a lot of great ones and of course *Seinfeld* and some of the others are up there — but there's never been a better television show than *Gunsmoke*. There would be cowboys and Indians, and I was always on the side of the Indians and, as I got to school, learned how to read and studied it a little more.

"My mom read a book to us, and it was kind of a scholarly book, which she had no business reading to children, about Geronimo, and we'd go slowly, explain it. So I started out with kind of a working knowledge of it at a surprisingly young age, like second grade, because she read the book to me and then I read stuff from there on and became fascinated by the ability of, not just Geronimo, but his people and the incredible things that they did. They routinely did stuff that people gasp at now days and did it while dodging bullets, too."

"HE SAT DOWN AND STARTED DOING SOME CARD TRICKS FOR ME. AND HE STARTED TELLING STORIES — ABOUT HIS LIFE, ABOUT WHAT HE'S RESEARCHED, ABOUT PIRATES. ONE STORY LEADS TO THE NEXT. I THINK MY DAD ASKED HIM HOW HE GOT INTO COACHING WITH A LAW DEGREE OR SOMETHING, AND THAT LED TO THE STORY ABOUT HIM MOVING TO FINLAND. NEXT THING YOU KNOW, HE'S TALKING ABOUT POLAND AND HOW SOME COUNTRY CHANGED LANGUAGES DURING WORLD WAR II, AND THAT'S WHY HE COULDN'T READ THE SUBTITLES. I DON'T KNOW WHAT HE WAS TALKING ABOUT."

— *Graham Harrell, on being recruited by Leach*

**12
Gig 'em**

"When he starts commenting about players of mine, that bothered me a little bit — (Stephen) McGee and that whole thing. He likes the rivalry. I think he liked the idea that he could get Aggies' goats when he wanted to . . . I enjoyed playing those games, yeah."

— **Mike Sherman**, Texas A&M coach,
recalling the Texas A&M-Texas Tech rivalry with Leach

While coaching at Texas Tech from 2000-2009, Mike Leach enjoyed the heated rivalry with Texas A&M perhaps more than with any other opponent. The spirit and tradition of Aggieland seemed to bring out the best in "Leachspeak."

He also enjoyed considerable success on the field, beating the Aggies seven out of ten times. That 7-3 mark included wins over three A&M head coaches — R. C. Slocum, Dennis Franchione, and Mike Sherman — and two overtime victories.

The games typically featured raucous crowds, whether it be at Jones SBC/AT&T Stadium in Lubbock or Kyle Field in College Station. In 2001, Mike McKinney, who was chief of staff at the time for Gov. Rick Perry, was at the game watching his son Seth, the A&M center. In a postgame melee that included the dismantling of the goalposts at Jones Stadium, the elder McKinney was punched and suffered facial cuts. He publicly blamed Tech officials (who admonished the students for their behavior), only to discover later that the assailant was actually an A&M student. Tech won that game, 12-0. (McKinney would go on to serve as chancellor of the Texas A&M System from 2006-2011.)

In a strange twist, the 2001 game carried over into the next year, when the A&M football media guide was published with disparaging remarks about Tech, calling Red Raider fans "classless clowns." Referring to the incident, the media guide stated, "Lubbock is ugly enough without any problems. The Raiders, even in victory, looked like classless clowns. No school in America better deserves Bobby Knight than Texas Tech."

"It was a lamentable mistake, for which a public apology already has been made," A&M president Robert Gates said. "I have directed the guide to be recalled and the offensive remarks removed before it is reissued (fifteen thousand of the media guides reprinted at a cost of $50,000)."

Not to be outdone, in 2007, a Tech fraternity was suspended for selling T-shirts with the image of the A&M mascot (Reveille, the dog) being hanged.

"A&M wants to rip on our fans and all that. Our fans are as good as their fans are. One thing our fans don't do is sit around and whine about other teams' fans. A&M spent a significant part of the week whining about what our fans are like. Why don't they worry about what themselves are like? There may be an individual or two that got out of hand. If someone commits criminal behavior . . . then that individual is responsible for it. It's interesting to me that all these Aggies — whether they're at A&M or here — are sitting around with halos over their heads and they have some divine expertise on fanmanship. I just don't believe that's the case. For the record, I think our fans are better than the Aggie fans."

— *Leach*

"I think we've got great fans, and I don't know what they're yelling and screaming. I've been to a lot of places on the road, and I don't recall any of them screaming anything nice."

— *Leach, on the Tech-A&M rivalry*

"I thought some of that was a bunch of foolishness. That's the excitement of college athletics. You go on the road, and it's tough to play on the road. Now everybody wants to entitle themselves to be touchy. I wanted it to be loud at Tech. I wanted it to be hostile at Tech, because, guess what? When I went on the road to Texas, Oklahoma, Oklahoma State, and, in particular, to Texas A&M, those were wild places to play. They were fun. I was excited every time we got to go to one of those stadiums because of the hostility of the crowd. If you were able to win the game, it was all the more rewarding. It was just an incredibly exciting place to be. Exciting environment. Everything about it was exciting. But, in the process, you can't be a baby about somebody calling you names."

— *Leach, on the "Raider Power" sportsmanship program at Texas Tech and the importance of a home-field advantage*

"Yeah, you've just got to work around the Corps. I think it's one of the greatest settings in college football, and they've got those guys with swords marching around."

*— **Leach**, on the atmosphere of playing at Texas A&M with the Corps of Cadets at Kyle Field*

"I'll make my annual plea that I think the opposing team should be given some swords, too, and, after the game, we'll give them back so the next opposing team can use the swords. I don't think it's fair that just one side should have swords. But I do think the Corps, in and of itself, is impressive. They march around there, and sometimes you have to dodge between columns to get to the locker room, but you work through that."

*— **Leach**, on playing at Texas A&M*

"How come they get to pretend they are soldiers? The thing is they aren't actually in the military. I ought to have Mike's Pirate School. The freshmen, all they get is the bandanna. When you're a senior, you get the sword and skull and crossbones. For homework, we'll work pirate maneuvers and stuff like that."

*— **Leach**, on the A&M cadets*

"I thought they did a pretty good job as far as pulling together. The one thing is, that's a hostile place to go, but I didn't feel like we had anyone who was intimidated. As far as effort and tempo, it didn't take us a quarter to warm up. We were firing bullets right away. Now they weren't always hitting what we were aiming at, but we were swinging away pretty well from the beginning."

*— **Leach**, on the performance of his Texas Tech freshmen in a 33-15 loss on the road at Texas A&M, 2000*

"I'm happy for Stephen McGee. The Dallas Cowboys like him more than his coaches at A&M did."

> — *Leach, on the Dallas Cowboys' drafting the A&M quarterback*

"I'M NOT ONE TO SAY THAT'S JUST MIKE BEING MIKE. YOU'RE NOT GOING TO GET A FREE PASS WITH ME. I DON'T GET A FREE PASS. I WOULD NEVER COMMENT ABOUT ANY OF HIS GUYS. HE CAN MAKE A JOKE ONCE IN A WHILE, AND EVERYBODY CAN LAUGH, BUT NOT AT OUR EXPENSE."

> — *Mike Sherman, Texas A&M coach,*
> *responding to Leach's comments about McGee*

"The remarkable thing is, all my life I've never been upset with the Aggies one time. They get upset with me anywhere from every four to six months. However, of all the times they've gotten upset with me, our fans, or anything I've said, it takes a heck of a detective to find something offensive in what I had to say about the draft."

> — *Leach*

"THAT COULD HAVE BEEN TAKEN AS A SHOT AT STEPHEN MCGEE, THAT IF HE WAS SO GOOD, THEN WHY DIDN'T HE PLAY? OR IT COULD HAVE BEEN TAKING A SHOT AT THE COWBOYS, OR AT (FORMER A&M COACH) DENNIS FRANCHIONE. COACH FRANCHIONE'S JOB WASN'T TO TRY AND MAKE STEPHEN AN NFL QUARTERBACK; IT WAS TO WIN FOOTBALL GAMES. AND IF IT WAS HIS FEELING THAT RUNNING THE FOOTBALL WAS HIS BEST CHOICE, LIKE IT WAS WHEN I WAS HERE (AS AN ASSISTANT) WITH R. C. (SLOCUM), THEN THAT'S WHAT HE DID."

> — *Sherman, again responding to Leach's comments*

"How can anyone not be shocked that they're offended by this? How is that possible? I mean, they're the ones that keep issuing these official statements. I haven't issued any official statement. I just answer questions when somebody asks me one."

*— **Leach**, responding to Sherman*

"This is a weird rivalry. One of the bizarre things was the accusation that we were spying on them. If that was the case, we would have played better."

*— **Leach**, after Tech's 33-15 loss to A&M in 2000.*
The Aggies had accused the Red Raiders of spying
on them at the Friday pregame walk-through.

"Tech always wants to beat A&M real bad and has for years. Is there some increment of more-bad we're supposed to want to beat them?"

*— **Leach**, when asked if the Tech-A&M*
rivalry had increased in intensity

"Once in awhile, a pirate can beat a soldier."

*— **Leach**, after Tech beat Texas A&M, 31-27,*
on a last-minute touchdown in College Station, 2006

13
Tattoos, Bobbleheads, and B12 Shots

"I've observed them in a very broad way over the years. Even though it's not really my cup of tea, there is a very creative element to it. I was asked if I wanted to get one (tattoo), but I said no. If I was interested in something, it would probably be a piercing because when I got tired of it, I could pull it out. And you don't have anything to look forward to with regard to me and piercing, believe me."

— **Leach**, on tattoos

Occasionally, no, make that frequently, Mike Leach's thoughts and comments veer off center and tend to defy categorization. Well-versed in most every subject, from history to current events to popular culture, Leach is a willing voice when it comes to expounding on most anything.

What coach other than Leach would be perfectly at ease discussing tattoos, jury duty, trick-or-treating, acoustics, his favorite belt, jeans, B12 shots, and bobbleheads?

"I think they should break that three-way tie based on graduation rates. I think the Big 12 conference should have an executive session (immediately). When they do that, they will find that no one's more deserving than the Red Raiders."

*— **Leach**, on the three-way tie in the Big 12 South between Texas Tech, Oklahoma, and Texas, 2008*

"Happy about it, but we talked about this: If everybody got one grade higher, if the whole group got one grade higher, we'd probably lead the nation. That's more within striking distance than a person would think. If you get somewhere between 2.9 and 3.0, 3.0 and change, you'll lead the nation in the public institutions. The privates? Who knows what kind of mischief they're up to? I mean, they hide their books and every-thing else, so they'd probably be a little more forthcoming if they weren't hiding something. So I think they warrant suspicion."

*— **Leach**, on Washington State's 2.66 fall semester grade-point average in 2013, the highest since the school began tracking such information in 1980*

"I was lucky in math — my last math class was sophomore (high school) geometry, and there are those that argue that geometry is not math."

*— **Leach***

"I had chemistry when I was a senior (in high school). I thought it'd be you'd do experiments and turn your buddy into Mr. Hyde. That didn't turn out to be the case. Instead, you sit there with a calculator and do a bunch of math. My teacher, at the time, I considered to be a total Nazi. But I knew I was going to college and I knew I had to pass, and I worked hard in that class."

*— **Leach***

"If you beat Nebraska in a game of marbles, that's a big deal."

— Leach

"Everybody's all surprised every time this stuff happens. It surprises me everybody gets surprised, because it happens every year like this, that there are surprises. The most surprising thing would be if there weren't any surprises. So, therefore, in the final analysis, none of it's really that surprising."

— Leach, on upsets in college football

"Occasionally, a player gets into some kind of bind and I have ideas, but mostly I use it to get out of jury duty."

— Leach, when asked if he applies his law degree to coaching

"Law school was different than undergrad, where you have a lot of fun because there are gorgeous girls running around and you can take all kinds of courses. In undergrad, if I didn't like a particular course, I'd just find something else. But law school was all law, all the time, and everyone there was pretty competitive."

— Leach, recalling his days in law school

"What happens with players, [it's] just like Judge Lance Ito gets in the middle of a big trial and decides it's more important for him to be a movie star than it is to be a judge. He had problems doing his [job] from one snap to the next. So if it can happen to good old Judge Ito, I'm sure it can happen to eighteen-to-twenty-two-year-olds."

— Leach, on his team not handling the limelight
well in a 41-10 loss to Missouri in 2007, comparing
it to the judge in the O. J. Simpson murder trial

At a weekly press conference:

Q: What are your thoughts on Christopher Columbus, and should he have a holiday?

Leach: "Well, being Scandinavian, I certainly think Christopher Columbus should get some credit. I don't have any problem with that, but I think we've got to make it Leif Erickson Day or Viking Day, so that would suit me if we got our day, as well. As we begin to diminish political correctness, we better get him pretty quick since we're inclined to make sure everybody's happy. But in Cody, Wyoming, as a kid, holiday significance was based on whether you got out of school or not. Well, we didn't get out of school, so I wasn't a big Columbus Day guy. You know, technically, Columbus never made it all the way to America. But it was impressive. It was like anything. A bunch of people told Columbus it couldn't be done, and he went and did it anyway."

On his Halloween costumes as a kid:

"My mom dyed a sheet and made a vampire outfit and had a really cool vampire cape. And the cape even had the little bat divots at the bottom of it, like their wings, and I was like the kid on *Calvin and Hobbes.* I was like Calvin, where when I put my outfit on, my personality would change. Since I was a vampire or Batman — depending on the scenario I had worked out in my mind — obviously there had to be criminals. Typically, that was my younger sister and brother and occasionally the neighbor kids. And so I would either have to fight crime or attack victims if I was a vampire.

"So that was a heck of a deal. I still have the cape somewhere. It doesn't fit anymore."

— Leach

"Over three incredibly productive years, he's grown quite attached to that helmet. We would definitely appreciate the safe return of that helmet, no questions asked. Please bring back Kliff's helmet."

> — *Leach, after Texas Tech quarterback Kliff Kingsbury's helmet disappeared after a game. The Lubbock Police later retrieved it and returned it to Kingsbury.*

"As we would talk among our friends, 'Let's go to the rich neighborhood.' Well that's a sucker bet all the way. There's far too much space between those houses. Rich people are at parties, they are not involved with Halloween. . . . You need to find three-bedroom communities with little space between the houses where there's a high volume of kids in those places, and those people will be involved in Halloween."

> — *Leach, on Halloween trick-or-treating strategy*

"Well, first of all, dentists that hand out toothbrushes, I don't like that; total rip-off. Apples, I can get those at home. I never had a problem with change (money). Candy corn, I hate. Candy corn is like the Halloween version of fruitcake. There's a reason it's only offered once a year — because it's horrible. Candy corn's awful.

"And the stuff in those Halloween wraps that are like rock-hard peanut-butter-tasting something or other, those are awful. Full-fledged candy bars, now that's a premium. I don't mean the short ones, but where they give you like a real candy bar, that's a biggie.

"Bubble gum was good if it was the round kind. I liked Jawbreakers, and Tootsie Pops were a little hard to beat. They were kind of standard, but it was always a pleasant surprise if it was a Tootsie Pop. Oh, Blow Pops, even a higher premium. . . . The best of the rest would have to be the Sprees, the little packets of Sprees."

> — *Leach, on his Halloween treats dislikes and likes*

"Probably the top item would be these packets of Airheads, you know, which are kinda these tangy, sweet, sort of chewy bars of stuff, which is pretty tough to go wrong with those. Although, I mean, dentists like them because they rot your teeth out, and they keep you in business."

— Leach, when asked what his family
distributed on Halloween, 2012

"I typically make the gravy. My wife, she does a good job cooking, but I'm far better at gravy than she is. . . . I put a lot of stuff into it. Once you understand the fact that you can't screw up gravy, the pressure is off. If it's not right, you just load it up with more water, milk, and occasionally flour, if it's not thick enough. And you can just start over — you can restart it all you want. . . . I think it's important to boil it down three times so everything's blended. I always put Tiger Sauce in mine."

— Leach, on fixing the gravy for
the family Thanksgiving meal

"It's the best of all worlds for your cholesterol."

— Leach, on mac and cheese pizza

"I don't know what a lentil is. Actually, despite not having a great deal of expertise on lentils, I did know there was a lentil festival here. I'll have to get to the bottom of this lentil stuff."

— Leach, on ordering a cup of lentil soup
and fish tacos at a Pullman restaurant

At a weekly press conference:

Q: Still been getting the green matcha at Café Moro (in Pullman, Washington)?

Leach: "I have. I kind of defer to him (chef) and he decides, you know. He decides and they stir stuff up. They've got the powder. It's all very mysterious. It's a lot like the medical profession. They wear white, cloaky stuff and then of course they have a stethoscope on that they never use and they write in illegible handwriting because they think it's not our business to see what it says and they'll stick it in Latin. And it's all just this pretentious charade of 'I'm the doctor and you're not,' so it's very similar to that."

"Barry Switzer understands, and this is an important point that's been lost in this metrosexual generation — there are not twenty-five types of jeans — there are two and they are either made by Levi's or Wrangler. And all that other stuff is slacks. Anybody that views anything else as jeans that extends beyond Levi's or Wrangler is simply incorrect, and Barry understands that in great detail."

— Leach

"I'm very big on cargo shorts. If it wouldn't create such a ridiculous national stir, I would love to be able to coach a game in shorts."

— Leach

"Right now, we (coaches) have a uniform just like they do at McDonald's and Burger King. You can tell a coach — especially when you go out recruiting — a mile away. I mean they've all got on the polo shirts and the khakis and the loafers — it's the most stereotypical thing in the world. They look like they're out of central casting. The unique guy has a visor on."

— *Leach*

"I would say one is I always wear my own belt. And the reason is because my belt's already broken in. So like they have these belts that college football, with rhinestone cowboy-looking belts, kinda took over with metal hardware. That just wasn't my style. I'm sure it looks great on some people. What is this? I've got a belt and there's this hunk of metal studded throughout the thing. So I didn't like those. I had another one that was kind of plastic-y and stiff. So I just screw this, I'm gonna just wear my belt. But that's more of a practical thing."

— *Leach*, *when asked about his pregame rituals*

"There was the asthma crew, of which I was the poster child. . . . (Acupuncture) worked tremendously, but the people I've tried to explain it to, tell it to, that also have asthma, to my knowledge, nobody's really taken me up on it, because they can't reconcile the needles."

— *Leach*

"We had a doctor that was giving B12 shots, and our strength coach (at Texas Tech) was really into B12 shots. So I'd get the B12 shot. And I guess we won the game or whatever when I got the first one. Then, after that, I had to hurry onto the field. I said, 'No, I don't have time for the B12 shot.' Bottom line is superstition existed with him and a couple other guys. Hey, part of the voodoo here is he has to get his B12 shot. So then it got to the point that I got the B12 shot more for them than for me just 'cause I didn't want a couple of nervous coaches. I wanted them settled down, and taking a B12 shot would be a small price to pay. You'd be surprised how many times there in the coaches' locker room, which is sort of separate and off to the side in Lubbock, I'd be bent over a table when the referees would come in, getting my B12 shot; some doctor's sticking a B12 shot in there so everyone got peace of mind and stuff."

— Leach, on more pregame rituals

"It's just the way my head is formulated. I gotta let it ride."

— Leach, on his unkempt hair

"For years, I've dyed it, thinking it would give me a more cerebral look rather than just some airhead thing. So I need to get a dye job to cover all that blond hair I've got going here."

— Leach, on his graying hair

"Cody is always throwing some sort of ball; there's always something whizzing by your head and a lot of scuffed walls in our house. I was more of a toy gun and G. I. Joe guy, but Cody definitely is more into balls and throwing them as much as he can."

— Leach, on life with his six-year-old son Cody, 2002

"The best dog I ever had was a terrier, like a mixed dog that we got from the pound. By far the best dog I ever had, not a breed that I necessarily would have selected, but we got it from the pound. . . . Labs are hard to beat. We always had black labs, but I don't think it matters what color. I like beagles, like the fact that they make a lot of noise, tick off the neighbors, but they don't age well. The older they get, they get fat bodies and little heads."

— Leach

"Red Raider fans are the best. Have kids and convert others."

— Leach

"It is amazing that people are talking to machines all the time. When I was a kid, my fantasy was always to get toys, even something as technologically advanced as Rock 'em, Sock 'em Robots, or the football game where it had the metal-vibrating thing that plugged in (electric football). . . . That was high-tech."

— Leach

"I'm not really good with technology. All this button pushing and whatnot. I mean, you can just imagine, based on what's happened in the last fifteen years, conversations won't happen ten years from now. There aren't going to be people to talk to, it's going to be this (mimics pushing buttons). 'Do you want to go out on a date with me?' 'I don't know, what do you look like?' 'Well, I look kind of like this.' 'OK, what are your interests?' 'Well, what do you think my interests are? Looking into this thing and typing into this, just like yours are.' 'Yeah, no kidding, that's what everybody's doing.' 'Well, where do you want to go?' 'Well, what difference does it make? Because all we're going to be doing is looking into machines anyways.' Well, that's true, and in the end, it's going to be tough to perpetuate the species. There's no question about that. So we're all going to look in this box and eventually be extinct. That's how it ends."

> — *Leach, on technology and life, at a press conference*

"Progress is a good thing, except for there's construction all the time."

> — *Leach*

"I've never gotten injured bad on rollerblades. There was a time I was bolting down a hill and a car comes, so then I pull out, basically into kind of a slide into the neighbor's lawn."

> — *Leach*

"I've got a walking thing going. It's 3.5 miles over the river and through the woods. It's about 3.5 miles to campus. I do all my phone calls. . . . I probably, on a slow day, between going there and back, it's seven miles round trip, and it's hilly here, too . . . it's worked out pretty good . . . kind of clears your mind a little bit. That's more important than you think. I get a little clarity going."

> — *Leach, talking about his daily walk in Pullman, Washington*

"There would be people that go in and jog, but I haven't. I raised it real high and I pretended I was walking on water one time."

> *— Leach, on the new underwater treadmill*
> *in the Washington State workout facility*

"I avoid golf. Golf is for people that need to improve on swearing. I don't need golf. . . . Later in my life maybe I will, but right now I don't."

> *— Leach*

"I hate golf. They should put magazine racks in the carts."

> *— Leach*

"These aren't like twirl-you-around, try-to-make-you-vomit deals. These are more like attractions. The technology on them alone is amazing."

> *— Leach, on his favorite theme park*
> *ride, the Pirates of the Caribbean*

"It's not everything it's cracked up to be because they'll dump water all over you and then you have to change your shirt, and that water is colder than you think. But you have to start working on win 101 tomorrow."

— *Leach, on celebrating after his one hundredth career win*

"You're all sticky. And I'll tell you the other thing: that stuff doesn't wash off half as easy as you might think. You find sticky spots like three days later."

— *Leach, on having Gatorade dumped on you instead of water*

"I would like to meet the caveman that invented a bobblehead because it's obviously been around a long time. I've never had a bobblehead I recall, maybe one handed out at a baseball game or something. No, actually, somebody gave me a Billy Martin bobblehead. Shoot, if it's good enough for Billy Martin, it's good enough for me. It's flattering, I just don't know how somebody would have thought of such a thing."

— *Leach, on the bobblehead of his likeness*
given to Washington State fans during a promotion

"I haven't given it much thought, but if they enjoy it and have fun with it, more power to them. It's more for wives and relatives than for me, 'cause every morning when I shave, I get the full effect. I don't shave every morning, so the full effect is not as meaningful as you might expect."

— Leach, on the bobblehead

"That marijuana thing is kind of interesting. All these people want to ban smoking, but they want to legalize marijuana? How about that?"

— Leach

At a weekly press conference:
Q: *Being that it's Thanksgiving and all, what are you thankful for this holiday season?"*
Leach: "They asked me that at the Tangerine Bowl, getting ready to play Clemson. So, it's me and Tommy Bowden. Actually they asked me what I wanted for Christmas. They're waiting for you to be greedier than hell and go, 'I want to win the bowl game.' So they're waiting for that. The pitfall of that occurred to me. So then I thought, what would Miss America do in this situation? I wished for world peace. So my Thanksgiving wish is for world peace."

From ESPN Live Chat with Mike Leach:
Q: *"What do you get asked most often by fans?"*
Leach: "Are you Mike Leach?"

14
Their Fat Little Girlfriends

"As coaches we failed to get through to them, and as coaches we failed to make our coaching points and our points more compelling than their fat little girlfriends. Now their fat little girlfriends have some obvious advantages. For one thing, their fat little girlfriends are telling them what they want to hear, which is 'how great you are,' and 'how easy it's going to be.' And we had a bunch of people who wanted to win the football game, but nobody wanted to play the football game. That defies every level of work ethic that exists with regard to football. As coaches we have to solve our failure on reaching them and the players have to listen. I am willing to go to fairly amazing lengths to make that happen."

— **Leach**, expressing his displeasure with the Red Raiders' lack of focus after an upset loss to Texas A&M

Mike Leach's comments regarding his players' "fat little girlfriends" following a loss to Texas A&M in October 2009 are arguably his most humorous and widely heard to date.

But, for the record, the Texas Tech coach had made a subtle reference to the subject (minus the "fat") six months earlier in the student newspaper, to little or no fanfare:

By Alex Ybarra
The Daily Toreador
Texas Tech coach Mike Leach believes his football team needs some more work after Tech's annual Red-Black game Saturday at Jones AT&T Stadium, so he told the players to expect another scrimmage

today in the last spring practice.

Leach lamented his first team offense and first team defense, adding that he was pleased with some of the younger players, as well as the second teams on both sides of the ball.

"(The first team was) just soft, bad effort, distracted with their nose in the newspaper," he said. "I don't know. (They) want to go see their little girlfriend and eat a fish sandwich under a shady tree. I don't know what their problem is. Maybe bad coaching, I don't know."

But back to the A&M game in the fall of '09.

To set the stage, after early-season losses to Texas and Houston, Tech had seemingly righted the ship, winning three games in a row (including a 31-10 pasting of nationally-ranked Nebraska). The team entered a home game against Texas A&M with a 5-2 record.

But in front of a shocked Jones AT&T Stadium crowd, the Red Raiders were thumped by the Aggies, 52-30.

Afterward, Leach was not amused by his team's apparent lack of focus, saying they were listening to their "fat little girlfriends," who were telling them how great they were instead of paying attention to their coaches. "Fat little girlfriends" analogies were interpreted any number of ways, but the bottom line was Leach was trying to get his team's attention. They noticed, as did the national media. Leach went on ESPN to explain his remarks, and while some might have thought his comments to be politically incorrect, most relished in the humor of it all.

Whatever the case, it seemed to work, as Tech won four of its last five games to finish with a 9-4 record. Unfortunately, Leach wasn't around to enjoy the Alamo Bowl win over Michigan State, having been terminated by the school over the alleged mistreatment of Adam James.

"You know, like I said, it starts with the coaching staff. But in the back of our minds as coaches, and in the back of our minds as players, well, ha-ha-ha, he-he-he, we pounded Kansas State. Kansas State pounded A&M. So, therefore, we're really going to pound Texas A&M."

— *Leach*

"HE'D MAKE A REALLY GOOD SPOKESMAN FOR JENNY CRAIG. I'VE NEVER HEARD A COACH SAY ANYTHING LIKE THAT."

— *Jimmy Kimmel, late-night TV talk show host, who showed a clip of Leach's "Fat Little Girlfriends" press conference*

ESPN College Football Live: *"Speaking of women, what was the best reaction to you questioning the reps the salad bar was getting from some of your players' girlfriends down at Texas Tech last weekend?"*

Leach: "I think the women in the state of Texas have a self-esteem that doesn't allow them to get upset about comments like that. And that's one of the great things about the state of Texas is the mental well-being of the women there.

"You know, figure of speech. When I first heard it, see, here's the full version of it. An offensive line coach I had the opportunity to work with one time at a camp, and I don't want to get him in any hot water — and I certainly don't feel like I'm in any, because we live in a great country that protects my rights to express myself freely.

"But what he used to originally say, and we've said it, too, is, you know, maybe he's upset. Maybe he's happy, I'm proud of you, you did this.

"Or you guys got to pick it up and do that. Then after that you can go sit under a tree with your fat little old girlfriend and have a fish sandwich and drink a lemonade.

"Well, so, that's kind of floated around our place for a while. And, you know, it's a figure of speech. You know, too high a level of relaxation. Too much listening to the outside. You know, so to those that are offended, I'm offended that you don't think I get to exercise my First Amendment rights, so that makes two of us. That's pretty much all I have to say about that.

"But I'm shocked that Jimmy Kimmel or any of these other people would even care what I have to say or what my opinion is on nearly every subject."

ESPNEWS: *"So how did 'fat little girlfriends,' how did that press conference play with your team in the locker room that week?"*

Leach: "I don't know how it played with (the players), but I thought we had really a good week as far as everybody listening and focused on their job and things like that. I think in football there's a lot of distractions. And when you have a group of, say, seventy guys that travel (to the games), each one of them has a certain level of distractions which affects how everybody can work together collectively.

"And I think that as a coach our message isn't the one you want to hear. Our message involves effort and working hard. Yeah, 'it's too bad that your legs are sore, but you need to do it any way.'

"Once they walk outside the locker room, the message is a little more positive and a little more patronizing, and I think it's one that's a little more appealing to listen to. And if you're not on-guard and don't put focus during football time, you may fall into the complacency that's provided by fat little girlfriends."

ESPNEWS: *You were going for a euphemism, right? You weren't going after one particular player as what may be happening with his relationship?*

Leach: "No, not one particular player. It's a metaphor for satisfaction, relaxation, and all that."

"I THINK THAT'S A BAD STATEMENT FOR THE RECRUITING OF TEXAS TECH. NO ONE WANTS TO GO THERE IF THEY HAVE FAT, LITTLE GIRL-FRIENDS. HERE AT KANSAS, OUR PLAYERS' ATTRACTIVE FEMALE GIRL-FRIENDS OR WHATEVER THEY ARE . . . FRIENDS — THEY'RE VERY SMART KU STUDENTS."

*— **Clint Bowen**, Kansas defensive coordinator*

"THEN THEY READ IT (PRESS CLIPPINGS) AND THEIR MOM READS IT AND THEIR DAD READS IT. THAT, AND THEIR *BEAUTIFUL* GIRLFRIENDS. YOU'VE GOT TO WORRY ABOUT ALL THAT."

*— **Pat Knight**, Texas Tech basketball coach, on his team's early success and the concerns he had with his team receiving recognition, 2009*

"QUITE HONESTLY, FOR A PROGRAM THAT WANTS TO WIN TEN GAMES OR MORE A YEAR, IT'S A CHALLENGE ENOUGH TO DO IT ON THE FIELD WITHOUT DISTRACTIONS. SO I'M NOT A FAN. I THINK THE GREATEST PIECE OF STRATEGY I EVER PLAYED UNDER WAS (COACH) RAYMOND BERRY IN NEW ENGLAND, AND HE USED THE OLD ADAGE THAT YOU JUST LAY LOW IN THE WEEDS AND LET EVERYONE ELSE DO THEIR THING AND THEN JUST COME OUT AND DO YOURS. I THINK IT'S NOT GOOD HAVING COMMENTS LIKE THOSE MADE."

*— **Craig James**, ESPN broadcaster, when The Oklahoman asked about Leach's remarks on fat little girlfriends, etc., November 13, 2009, about six weeks before Leach was fired*

"I think they're deliberately taunting us, and I think that that's something our players should make note of and perhaps use for motivation as opposed to listening to their fat little girlfriends."

— *Leach, joking about facing Kansas and a Jayhawk defensive back named Lubbock Smith*

"And then after I looked at the (game) film, I realized it's far worse than I first thought. Their girlfriends are fatter than I first thought, and there's more of them."

— *Leach, asked if he ever thought about apologizing after reflecting on his remarks, 2011*

"THERE'S PRETTY GIRLS EVERYWHERE. TECH'S GOT THEIR SHARE, KU HAS THEIR SHARE. WE'RE PARTIAL. WE THINK KU HAS THE BEST. I THINK YOU CAN HAVE FUN WITH IT. THAT'S WHAT MIKE IS TRYING TO DO."

— *Mark Mangino, Kansas coach*

"I've yet to meet anybody that was ticked off about that comment."

— *Leach, in 2011, reflecting on his "fat little girlfriends" quote*

"I would like to have a dollar for every time somebody said something about how many points we were going to score or how bad we were going to beat them, you know, how great we are, and how good everything looks. Well, it's all a bunch of crap. I told this to the team, if you don't learn from somebody else's mistakes in history, you're destined to repeat them, which is essentially what we did."

— *Leach, on the upset loss to Texas A&M, 2009*

"If you have a ridiculously weak opponent, you might play bad and overpower them, but you can't do that against a tradition and a program like Texas A&M. If it was easy, anybody could do it. If it was easy, I'd be coaching the Swedish bikini team and I'd have them coming out here to do all this."

— ***Leach****, on the upset loss in 2009*

"Any time they get stroked, they want to beam over it like they got an *A* on their report card and they're going to get an extra quarter to go buy an ice cream cone."

— ***Leach****, on his players' reacting to positive media coverage*

"I think, as a team, we're not mentally tough enough to deal with positive reinforcement. I think, as a team, we like pats on the back more than we like being focused on the task at hand and doing what we need to do. We're in this vicious circle of — we get stroked, feel good, get drilled, and then play well, you know. We need to be a mentally tougher team."

— ***Leach***

"We had an offense that was extremely powerful, extremely productive, that probably sits and reads their press clippings in an arrogant fashion, sat around the sideline with their arms folded for most of the second half. And then, defensively, the entire first half, we got hit in the mouth and acted like somebody took our lunch money. All we wanted to do was have pouty expressions on our face until somebody dabbed our little tears off and made us feel better. And then we go out there and try harder once our mommies told us we were okay. Well, neither one of those things was acceptable. They think concerned expressions are a replacement for fast legs, low pads, and determined effort. That's not acceptable. It was pitiful. It was flat-out

Mike Leach's Texas Tech teams enjoyed a true home field advantage during his ten years in Lubbock. Under Leach, the Red Raiders won 53 of 64 games played at Jones SBC/AT&T Stadium.

pitiful. We're some vaunted offense, so we're going to sit here with our arms folded. Oh, well, we'll have three lackadaisical plays, and then we'll punt and make it the defense's problem. Well, that's incredibly soft and incredibly front-runnerish."
— ***Leach***, *after Texas Tech's poor showing against Oklahoma State, 2007*

"The defense can't sit there and pout. The other guy, he scores or does something, lower your pads, run your feet, get mean and nasty."
— ***Leach***

"I tell you what I was starting to get sick of was some guy getting depressed and moping around because he made a bad play. We've been having too much of that guy acts like he's ready to go, and they get the little moping face going, and then, yeah, we don't have time to sit and wait for that. We didn't really have big problems with somebody, you know, sometimes a guy gets overexuberant if he makes a play and it takes a series or two to get them back. We didn't have a problem with that. Somebody would make a mistake, and then everybody else was going to wait on him to mope about it for a series or so. And I thought there was too much of that."

— *Leach, on an improved attitude*

"For two-thirds of the game, we played real well. The last third, we faced adversity and waved the white flag. . . . I don't know if they all had dentist's appointments or what, but these games are sixty minutes."

— *Leach, after seeing his team take a seven-point lead in the third quarter, only to be outscored 35-0 the rest of the game*

"Utah's team deserves a lot of credit. They're not that good; we're not that bad. Despite what the score was, they could have beat us by a hundred today."

— *Leach, after Washington State's 49-6 loss to Utah, 2012*

"TCU deserves some credit, and I'll be nice and politically correct about that. But that was the sorriest offensive effort I have ever seen. Today I coached the worst offense in America, which makes me the worst offensive coach in America."

— *Leach, after Texas Tech's loss to TCU, 12-3, 2006*

"I saw a bunch of prima donna pretty boys prancing around like they were too good to be there. And then when we got hit in the mouth, they looked surprised and frustrated, like this isn't supposed to happen. . . . Like didn't (the Tech players') press agent talk to TCU and let them know how good they were and what they did last year? Then they got frustrated like they were too good to fight back. I mean, we didn't even fight back. We went out there and [TCU] was tougher than we were. We were soft, and [had] our pretty boy little attitude . . . we got what we deserved."

— *Leach, after the loss to TCU*

"I'm willing to replace them with people that may not be as talented at this point as long as they play hard. If somebody plays hard and practices hard, they're going to start this week. I'm not messing with any of these frontrunner showboats that I've tolerated. Long story short, I'm either going to have to replace them or change them. Our biggest failure is a lack of effort. That's what is disturbing. About half of what I'd like to do to address this is illegal."

— *Leach, on some of his starters*

"We've got big heads and we're not tough enough to go out there and make plays. I don't know if it's big heads or we're scared. I'm kind of curious: are they scared or do they have big heads? Right now, they're nothing special. And it's a by-product of my coaching and other people's coaching. We're nothing special, not at quarterback or receiver. We can pretend we are."

— *Leach, upset, even though Texas Tech blasted SMU, 43-7*

"I think some of that existed, but I don't think I addressed it real well. The best way is the way that gets the best results. I don't think that got the best results, so that's not the best way."

> — *Leach, questioning if he was too critical of his players after a loss to TCU.*

"They waited for us to stand there and wet our pants, apparently."

> — *Leach, on how Colorado slowed down the prolific Tech offense*

"We're not tough enough to step up there and play to our ability because all we want to do is talk about what happened against Nebraska. Everybody wanted to coast around and look at the other guy and see what he was going to do. It's just a bunch of sheep looking around staring at one another."

> — *Leach, displeased with his Red Raiders after a 51-21 loss to Texas. Two weeks earlier, Tech had thrashed Nebraska, 70-10.*

"They need to take accountability. I'm tired of going out there and seeing everybody react as a herd, you know. Some of the cows in the herd need to be bigger than the other ones, and, right now, we're battling for that. We're battling for that in a big way."

> — *Leach, after the Nebraska loss*

"A bunch of times, we have a bunch of people talking about it, and they get an angry look on their face and think that covers intensity. That isn't intensity. Intensity is what follows the angry look, not just the angry look. Right now, we're just as far as the angry look."

> — *Leach, on a lack of intensity*

"Nobody truly knows what went on in Kansas. But my suspicion is Mark's in the middle of a witch hunt, which is unjustified. Heaven forbid somebody should ask the guys to pay attention and focus in, and for the sake of all his teammates and coaches and everybody else, pay attention. Well, there's different ways to ask a guy to do that, and sometimes after you've asked him a number of times, you raise the bar. . . . The interesting thing to me is all the (reports) went from (Mangino) hit some guy in the face to, 'Well, he didn't even touch anybody, but he did say mean things to them. . . . ' A mean man told some players something they didn't want to hear. Well, there's a mean man in Lubbock who tells people stuff they don't want to hear, too, and that's part of it."

*— Leach, on Kansas forcing the resignation
of football coach Mark Mangino, 2009*

"Right now, as a team, we don't know if we walk to school or carry our lunch. If you can do it once, why can't you do it every time? They're just too quick to relax, want to enjoy the good life."

— Leach, after an inconsistent practice

"If you really wanted to see us play well, you should have been there for Monday's practice."

— Leach, after a disappointing 30-6 loss to Brigham Young

"We played in kind of a celebratory fashion, which is really disturbing to me. At some point, we're going to have to purge that if we're going to improve as a football team."

— Leach, after Texas Tech's 31-27 victory over Texas A&M, 2006

"We don't have time to pout. I'm not putting up with pouters. We've got to fix it and become the best team that we can and play a full sixty minutes."

— *Leach*, *after Texas Tech's 49-45 loss to Oklahoma State, 2007*

"They (the Red Raiders) are always looking for a rest area in the road. I mean, they'll cruise down the highway and they'll stop. You know, 'Let's coast. We did something good, so now let's coast.' That's just a horrible mentality. It's weak. . . . I'm going to spend the whole week trying to strangle the first guy that's got that goofy little smile like we accomplished something. 'Oh, we accomplished something! Let's yuk it up and pat each other on the back, and, oh, what memories it'll create!' That drives me crazy."

— *Leach*, *after a sloppy Texas Tech victory over Baylor, 2004*

"Hell, we're only playing with five. I worry about all our freshmen and sophomores getting so excited for the seniors that they'll be so over-wrought with their emotions that they may not bring it all together."

— *Leach*, *sarcastically, when asked about the emotions of Senior Day, in which Texas Tech started only five seniors*

"And then we kind of have distracted focus, and we have a certain amount of satisfaction. I think there's still a certain amount that exists on our team that the team that wins is the one that has the most fun, and as long as there's a treat at the end and everybody has a good time and gets to wear the same T-shirt, we're all happy. Well, that's not the case, and that's really not how I view college football. And so I think there's a difference in philosophy. In some cases, it's going to have to be changed."

— *Leach*, *on his first Washington State team, 2012*

"How many people have ever really had fun when they didn't give great effort? I mean, if you're some screwy party guy, I mean, the guys that have the most fun are the ones that try the hardest, you know."

— *Leach, talking to his team at practice about effort*

"HE SAID, 'EVEN LITTLE OLD LADIES CAN GIVE EFFORT. THEY MAY NOT GET GREAT RESULTS, BUT THEY CAN GIVE GREAT EFFORT.'"

— *Deone Bucannon, Washington State safety,*
quoting Leach during a lethargic practice

"Our effort today was pitiful. It starts with our coaches. Our coaches, me in particular, it starts with me, starts with my assistants, we need to be able to reach our players, get good effort. Shoot, a part of it's effort, and some of it borders on cowardice. Our five (offensive linemen) couldn't whip their two (defensive linemen). Sometimes they brought two. Our five couldn't whip two. If five of our guys went in an alley and got in a fight with two of theirs, we would have gotten massacred. That's just ridiculously inexcusable. It was one of the most heartless efforts I've ever seen, and our D-line wasn't any better."

— *Leach, after a 49-6 Washington State loss to Utah, 2012*

"I don't know if somehow they think there's some level of accomplishment in that, which there's not because we still lost last week, last time I checked, and there's plenty of ways we could have played better last week. If we're taking satisfaction out of last week, we're out of our mind. Not one play last week counts for this week. So, no, right now we're a team that doesn't give good effort, which means all the stuff we do in the weight rooms, meeting rooms, practices, we're wasting our time if we're not going to give good effort. We're going to be working on effort this week."

*— **Leach**, after the loss to Utah and reflecting on a narrow loss the week before*

"I don't know how the hell we aren't awake. I mean, the wealth of wins that we've enjoyed around here, so we're not awake? We've got this rich tradition of kicking everyone's ass, so we're not awake? How can you not be awake? I'm not saying you're wrong. The saddest thing of all is that I suspect you're right."

*— **Leach**, when asked if blowing a fourth-quarter lead to Colorado might serve as a wake-up call for his Washington State team*

"We'll get something figured out. I don't know. If you figure it out, give me a call. Because I can't fathom on any level how you work at anything and then come out and just not even try. It doesn't matter what physical condition a person's in, how old, how young, anybody is capable of great effort. Anybody is capable of it. The fact of the matter is, today we refused to give it."

*— **Leach**, when asked how you work on effort*

On what the coaches were not getting through to the players:
"If lesson one, Pee-Wee football lesson one, is effort. We're responsible for this team and, for whatever reason, we haven't had the ability to convey great effort. Not to the point it stuck that we had any great effort plays today. I don't recall any."

*— **Leach***

"If you have to beg an eighteen-to-twenty-two-year-old kid to give good effort, then you've got the wrong kids on your team."
— *Leach, after the Utah loss*

"We'll consider anything. If I found anyone who quit on the film, I might consider cutting them on the spot."
— *Leach, after Texas Tech's poor effort on offense and special teams in a loss to Colorado, 2002*

"I think we had good effort, but it was frantic, like over-pursuing. Fighter pilots always say you want to be one inch out of control. We were about six inches."
— *Leach, after Washington State's 46-7 loss at Arizona State, 2012*

"It's not just a group of, like, picnics and softball games or nothing, but the business of players being together. Also, we (coaches) get too caught up on what we're doing rather than bring a guy in the office and pat him on the back because there's a lot more to this than Xs and Os. You're dealing with people and people working together."
— *Leach, on a "splintered" team, in part because he and other Texas Tech coaches hadn't given players opportunities to spend time together, after a loss to Colorado, 2006*

"When, as a team, collectively, we believe we're a good team, we will play better. There's way too much salesmanship going into, you know, 'Oh, but really you are a good team. Oh, yes, you are.' That's a bunch of crap. At some point, a guy's got to get out there and say, 'I worked hard at this and it means something to me and I'm going to prevail over my opposition,' rather than all these little boosts and dust-offs and pats on the back, everybody feels good, we're crazy on that thing. We're more concerned about relationships and people being happy than performance. Until we put performance in front of all that, it's going to take a while. We can make the decision and do it today, or we can drag our feet. But right now, our players, coaches, and everybody that it's meaningful to, we need to get those other guys on board. Either that or get them out of here."

— *Leach, on Washington State's attitude*

"We just need to address ourselves and go out there and make things happen. We really need to knock off all our, you know, 'touchy, feely, get in touch with our feelings and twelve-step program' mentality around here."

— *Leach, after Texas Tech's 51-21 loss to Texas*
and preparing to play at Kansas State, 2004

"You want a good sideline atmosphere. You want them cheering for their teammates. For nine years, I provided so much seating for everybody, it was kind of contrary to what I was telling them to do. You know, 'Here, sit down.' No, I want you to stand up.

"I like it quite a lot. Heck, I stand the whole game. God forbid that an eighteen-to-twenty-two-year-old athlete should have to go stand and cheer his teammates out there. I think we all like it.

"We've got a little more seating than is necessary, but between series, as you're trying to make corrections, it provides a good gathering point, whether anybody sits on it or not."

— Leach, on limiting the bench seating to starters only at Texas Tech

"That's just an excuse. They can generate their own enthusiasm. We can issue party favors before the game or something like that. They need Sheffield for enthusiasm, and Sheffield does a great job of that, no question. But somebody else, they need to have their own damn enthusiasm.

"We travel seventy people to this game that can generate their own enthusiasm, and the fact that they have been at this for years and years and years should be reason for enthusiasm enough. Any mopey-whininess, we will go roll around in some damn sand and see if that is enthusiasm. Those guys whining about enthusiasm can get off their (butts) and be enthusiastic."

— Leach, rebuking senior players who suggested the
team missed the enthusiasm of injured quarterback
Steven Sheffield, who had directed Texas Tech to a three-game
winning streak, but was on the sidelines on crutches during a loss

15
Empty Corpses and Zombies

"I think it's mixed. I think some of it's stellar. Some of them have been great and some of them have been very poor. Some of them have had kind of this zombie-like, go-through- the-motions, everything is like how it's always been, that's how it'll always be. Some of them quite honestly, have an empty-corpse quality. That's not pleasant to say or pleasant to think about, but that's a fact. That's why it's been necessary for us to have the youth movement that we've had."

— **Leach**, after his team started 2-4, when asked about senior leadership at Washington State in 2012

One of the biggest challenges Mike Leach faced when taking the Washington State job in 2012 was changing the mindset and culture of a football program that had not experienced a winning season since 2003. Such change is often slow and painful.

Leach's "zombies and corpses" quote generated a great deal of media attention, but at the same time, might have awakened some of the players, *a la* "fat little girlfriends." At the very least, the comments made clear that to be successful, the team was going to have to buy into Leach's tough love philosophy. This includes such variables as attitude, leadership, work ethic, physical endurance, academics, and discipline.

As would be expected, several players left the team during the first year, including a star receiver who claimed he and others were mistreated by the coaches. Subsequent investigations uncovered no such mistreatment. By the end of the 3-9 season, Leach's message seemed to be sinking in, as the Cougars ended on an upswing with an upset win over Washington in the Apple Cup.

"That could have been a zombie convention out there."
— *Leach, on his players after Washington State's 49-6 loss to Utah, 2012*

"The biggest thing, most of our leadership's coming from younger guys. We do have some key seniors that really do a good job. And it's interesting that somebody told me about a quote that was taken out of context, which certainly wouldn't be the first time they've taken something I said out of context, but at any rate, we've got some seniors doing a good job. We've got a whole bunch of them, as I said, are dead corpses. You can either breathe life into yourself and get out there and play. . . . We've got a bunch of younger guys that are stepping up and playing hard."

— *Leach*

"I don't regret saying it. I was actually trying to make a point about how great some of the seniors have been, and I singled out several of them. But, for some guys, it's very hard. One of the things you try to teach is that you and your team can make progress on every play — regardless of score, regardless of record. I know that can be tough to buy into when you've been losing and you've been disappointed in the past. These guys started every single season of their careers thinking they were going to win and then it crashed on them. We're struggling, and they can see that the end isn't that far away. Some have handled that great, others haven't. I can tell the difference by the way they look in practice, in meetings, in games. That was the point I was making. I wasn't saying any of them are bad kids. I was saying it's very tough for all of them, which is why I admire the guys who *have* been able to avoid that mentality so much."

— *Leach*

"I get asked about my evaluation in this business, and it's said a bunch. These things, typically, if I say them at all or if they're even quoted in context, I say them once, and that certainly wasn't the entire gist of the quote. That may be how you took it and so, honestly, there really wasn't much of a question in there, more of an editorial comment on your part, so you go ahead and write whatever you feel good about."

— *Leach*

"It's funny, this day and age people ask questions, but they don't always want honest answers. In the midst of that, I mean, you know, if somebody is a zombie or corpse, I'm the head zombie or corpse. Anything with regard to a team effort or coaching, if you don't like the way your players are playing, that's about how well you're coaching, you know?"

— *Leach, reflecting on his empty corpse/zombie quote, at Pac-12 Media Day, 2013*

"We just saw a lot of ghosts, rather than go ahead and play and isolate our job or responsibilities against the guy across from us. We made more out of it than there was. All of a sudden we're going through a bunch of mental gyrations about how this is the No. 1 team in the nation, or, 'Ooh, this is Nebraska,' all this irrelevant stuff that doesn't apply."

— *Leach, after Texas Tech lost to Nebraska, 56-3, 2000*

"There's also some individuals that aren't going to be here next year. When we get off the plane, as coaches, we're going to meet and we're going to discuss and adjust our approach and figure out what we're going to do throughout the week."

— *Leach, after Washington State's 49-6 loss to Utah*

"The older guys are a little more defeatist. The younger guys have a little more 'I am freshman; hear me roar' type of thing."
— Leach, reflecting on his first season at Washington State

"If a player doesn't like the way something is going, he can quit. Or go find him a team where they don't coach very hard, or where lackadaisical effort is allowed. People don't join football or coach football to see people go out and be lazy. If they wanted it to be comfortable, they wouldn't call it football. They'd call it cuddling."
— Leach

"As coaches, you put pressure on yourself to improve, because ultimately the blame lies there. Anybody that's not on board, you get rid of them. It doesn't matter if it's a player or a coach or somebody in the background.... if they're not on board, you get rid of them."
— Leach

"We didn't play hard. We weren't tough at all. It's a problem, and it will be addressed in the off-season. We're going to have a hell of an off-season to address this. I mean, why go out and not play hard? It's the most stupid thing I've seen in my life."
— Leach, after Texas Tech's 40-27 loss to East Carolina in the 2001 galleryfurniture.com bowl

16
Leach

"What you see is what you get. He's sure not pretentious in any way — he's Mike."

> — **Grant Teaff**, executive director of the American Football Coaches Association, on Leach, 2011

Eccentric. Eclectic. Unique. Unconventional. Intellectual. Quirky. Humorous. Unorthodox.

Mike Leach is all of these things and more.

His personality, interests, and coaching style have also led to a number of monikers.

"The Pirate." "The Mad Professor." "The Strange One." "The Mad Genius." "Captain Mike." "Mad Mike." "Columbo." "The Mad Scientist."

Again, Mike Leach is all these and more.

"The best thing about this coaching stuff is it saved me from being an attorney. I've been coaching for twelve years now. So guys I graduated with are jealous of what I do when I go to work every day, and I'm jealous of the fact they drive Mercedes Benzes and buy condominiums."

— *Leach, 1999*

"I have a low-pitched voice, though. One time when a person mistook me for Vince Gill, this is after it had happened a couple of times, finally, she says, 'Your voice sounds different.' I said, 'Yeah, it's more high-pitched when I sing.'"

— *Leach*

Scott Pelley (60 Minutes)*: "One sportswriter called you a football madman directing a sideshow."*

Leach: "Um, yeah, well, I don't know . . . I don't have any disagreement with it, really."

Radio interviewer: "I always thought you were like, six (foot) four. You come off as a big guy when we see you on TV."

Leach: "I get that a lot. . . . No, I'm exactly this size. Well, I have a fat face, maybe that contributes to it."

"MIKE WAS DIFFERENT. WE HAD ALWAYS HAD WEST TEXAS GUYS. WE ALWAYS RAN THE BALL HERE. THE FIRST TIME MIKE'S OFFENSE CAME OUT ON THE FIELD EVERYONE IS LIKE, 'WHOA.' HE HAS THAT PLAY HE CALLS THE NINJA — WHEN THEY ALL LINE UP ON ONE END. I'M NOT SURE ANYONE HAD EVER SEEN THE NINJA. IT WAS JUST A SHOCK EFFECT. MIKE'S PERSONALITY WAS LIKE THAT, TOO."

— *Patty Ross, long-time Texas Tech football administrative assistant*

"HE'S GOT ABOUT A DOZEN DIFFERENT PERSONALITIES. HE'S A MAD SCIENTIST, A COMEDIAN, A STORYTELLER ALL ROLLED INTO ONE. I GUESS THE BEST DESCRIPTION IS THAT HE'S AN ENTERTAINER."

— *Cody Hodges, former Texas Tech quarterback*

"IT'S HARD TO FIND IN COLLEGE FOOTBALL, BUT MIKE IS AUTHENTIC. HE'S NOT TRYING TO BE ANYBODY HE'S NOT. AND I THINK EVERYBODY WHO WORKS FOR HIM APPRECIATES THAT, AND PLAYERS APPRECIATE THAT, AND I THINK THAT'S A BIG REASON HE'S SUCCESSFUL. HE'S NOT AFRAID TO BE DIFFERENT, TO TRY SOMETHING NOBODY ELSE IS DOING. HE IS WHO HE IS, COMPLETELY AUTHENTIC."

— *Sonny Dykes, former Texas Tech*
assistant and now head coach at California

"MIKE IS LIKE A MAD SCIENTIST, AND HE'S GOING TO DO IT HIS WAY. SOMETIMES YOU MIGHT THINK, 'WHAT IS HE DOING?' BUT, BELIEVE ME, THERE'S A REASON FOR EVERYTHING HE DOES. HE'S A LITTLE OFFBEAT, BECAUSE HE MARCHES TO A DIFFERENT DRUMMER, BUT THAT'S THE WAY HE WANTS TO BE. . . . I'M TELLING YOU, HE'S A CHARACTER — A LOT OF FUN, AND A BIT OFF THE WALL — BUT HE'LL FIT LIKE A GLOVE IN PULLMAN. HE'S A JEANS-AND-T-SHIRT KIND OF GUY. HE'S BEEN AROUND AND DONE IT AT BIGGER PLACES, BUT HE'LL ENJOY THE HECK OUT OF PULLMAN, AND PULLMAN WILL ENJOY THE HECK OUT OF HIM."

—*Mike Price, UTEP coach and a former*
Washington State coach, on the Cougars' hiring of Leach, 2012

"THEY CALL HIM A MAD SCIENTIST, BUT HE'S MORE OF A MAD ARTIST. HE'S A THINKER. MIKE LEACH IS SITTING THERE ALMOST LIKE A BIRD-WATCHER, WAITING FOR SOMETHING TO HAPPEN SO HE CAN THINK ABOUT WHAT THAT MEANS. AND THE PLAYERS, THEY FEEL LIKE

THEY'VE WALKED INTO THE FUNHOUSE. THEY COME OUT OF HIGH
SCHOOL AND, ALL OF A SUDDEN, THEY FIND THEMSELVES ON FOURTH-
AND-SIXTEEN IN THEIR OWN TERRITORY, AND THE COACH IS SENDING
IN A PLAY. IT LIBERATES THE PLAYERS."

—Michael Lewis, author who profiled
Leach in New York Times Magazine

"UNDER ALL THE LAUGHING AND HUMOR, HE IS A TREMENDOUS FOOT-
BALL COACH. YOU GET HIM AWAY FROM FOOTBALL, AND HE'S ONE OF
THE MOST ENJOYABLE GUYS I'VE BEEN AROUND. HE IS A DANDY — UN-
DERLINE THAT ONE. HE'S A REAL SMART GUY — A REAL SMART GUY. HE
WALKS TO THE BEAT OF A DIFFERENT DRUMMER. BUT HE'S BRILLIANT."

— Dan McCarney, Iowa State coach , 2006

"I LOVE WORKING FOR MIKE. IT WAS A NO-BRAINER WHEN HE ASKED
ME TO WORK FOR HIM. I WILL TELL YOU MIKE IS A PLAYER'S COACH.
. . . SECONDLY, MIKE IS A FAMILY GUY. I APPRECIATE THAT. PEOPLE
DON'T REALIZE IT, BUT HE'S A CHEVY CHASE VACATION-TYPE GUY. HE
MAKES EVERY ONE OF US TAKE A CHEVY CHASE VACATION. AND IF
WE DON'T, HE HAS US GO WITH HIM. THAT'S THE TRUTH."

— Ruffin McNeill, Texas Tech defensive coordinator

"HE IS SCARILY GENIUS. I THINK HE'S A GOOD MAN WITH A GOOD PHI-
LOSOPHY. I THINK HE'S JUST WHAT TEXAS TECH NEEDS. HE'S GETTING
BETTER AT DEALING WITH THE MEDIA. . . . HE WORKED IN OBSCURITY
AS AN OFFENSIVE COORDINATOR FOR A LONG TIME AND IS DOING BET-
TER AT COMMUNICATING. WHAT I LIKE ABOUT HIM IS THAT HE'S HON-
EST. YOU'LL GET WHAT HE'S THINKING, NOT COOKIE-CUTTER REMARKS."

— Emily Jones, Lubbock sportscaster, 2003

"HE'S SO HONEST. HE'S NOT PARANOID. HE'S JUST A NEAT GUY TO TALK TO, THE KIND OF GUY YOU'D LIKE TO SIT NEXT TO AND HAVE A BEER WITH — AND AT THE SAME TIME YOU'D LEARN A LOT OF FOOTBALL."

— *Thom Brennaman, broadcaster, on interviewing Leach*

"FROM THE BROADCASTING SIDE, I THINK HE'S A WELCOME RELIEF TO THE VANILLA — SOMETIMES (COACHES) ARE AFRAID OF THE MEDIA."

— *Rick Neuheisel, broadcaster and former coach, on Leach*

"MIKE LEACH PUTS ACADEMICS FIRST IN HIS PROGRAM. THESE YOUNG MEN ARE STUDENTS FIRST. MIKE IS A FIRST-CLASS COACH WHOSE TEAMS BRING HONOR TO TEXAS TECH BOTH ON THE FIELD AND IN THE CLASSROOM."

— *Jon Whitmore, Texas Tech president, 2006*

"MIKE IS MIKE. HE SPEAKS HIS MIND, AND HE'S ENOUGH OF AN INDI-VIDUAL THAT GOES WITH HIS OWN DRUMMER THAT IT DOESN'T LOOK LIKE HE'S ANOTHER COACH. OUR NO. 1 PURPOSE IS AN EDUCATIONAL INSTITUTION AND HIGHER LEARNING, AND HE PROMOTES OUR PUR-POSE."

— *Kent Hance, Texas Tech chancellor, November 23, 2009*

"MIKE'S THE TYPE OF GUY, HE SPEAKS WHAT HE'S THINKING, TO SOME DEGREE, I THINK IT'S GOOD. YOU CAN'T ACCUSE HIM OF BEING A HYP-OCRITE. HE TELLS IT LIKE IT IS."

— *Mark Mangino, Kansas coach*

"ANY TIME YOU HAVE SOMEBODY WHOSE NAME IS ASSOCIATED WITH YOUR INSTITUTION IN A POSITIVE WAY, THAT'S A VERY HELPFUL THING. MIKE HAS DONE SOME GREAT THINGS ON THE FIELD. WHEN PEOPLE THINK MIKE LEACH, THEY THINK TECH. THE OTHER THING THAT'S SO HELPFUL ABOUT HIS NAME IS THAT HE'S ASSOCIATED WITH ACADEMIC INTEGRITY AND ACADEMIC SUCCESS."

— *Guy Bailey, Texas Tech president, November 23, 2009, about a month before Leach was fired*

"SOMETIMES, MIKE'S OUT THERE A LITTLE FAR FOR YOU TO LATCH ONTO. BUT HE'S REALLY A GREAT GUY. HE COMMUNICATES WITH THE PLAYERS; HE KNOWS WHEN TO JUMP ON THEM AND WHEN TO BACK OFF. HE CAN COACH."

— *E. J. Holub, Texas Tech's first All-American*

"HE CAME TO MY HOUSE TO VISIT WHEN HE STARTED RECRUITING ME, AND I REALLY DIDN'T KNOW WHAT TO EXPECT. I WAS SITTING WITH HIM ON THE COUCH AND HAVING A CONVERSATION WHEN HE REAL-IZED WE HAD AN AB WHEEL (AN EXERCISE APPARATUS) ON THE FLOOR. SO IN THE MIDDLE OF THE CONVERSATION HE GETS ON THE GROUND AND STARTS TRYING TO USE IT WHILE ASKING ME QUESTIONS."

— *Josh Rangel, former Texas Tech safety, recalling a recruiting visit from Leach*

"IT WAS A THREE-HOUR LUNCH, AND I'M THINKING, 'WELL, ARE WE GOING TO GET AN OFFER HERE OR WHAT?' (LEACH IS) THERE, AND HE'S EATING THESE STRAWBERRIES THE SIZE OF APPLES."

— *Leland Welker, recalling when he and his son, Wes, met Leach for the first time and Wes being offered a scholarship*

"WHEN COACH COMES TO VISIT FOR RECRUITING, IT'S AN EXPERIENCE LIKE NONE OTHER. IT'S MAGIC TRICKS AND STORY TIME. PEOPLE THINK: 'WELL, MAYBE ONCE YOU'VE BEEN AROUND HIM FOR FIVE YEARS, IT'S NOT NEAR AS AMUSING.' BUT IT IS. HE COMES UP WITH NEW STORIES AND RESEARCHES NEW TOPICS."

— *Graham Harrell*, *former Texas Tech quarterback*

"COACH LEACH IS JUST HIMSELF. IT COULD BE TWENTY-FIVE DEGREES AND SNOWING IN LUBBOCK, AND HE'S COME IN WEARING FLIP-FLOPS AND SHORTS. HE'S JUST A CHARACTER. HE WAS A GOOD COACH, THOUGH. HE WAS VERY LAID BACK."

— *Colby Whitlock*, *former Texas Tech defensive lineman*

"IF YOU TALK TO THE GUY, YOU'LL SEE HE'S ON ANOTHER LEVEL IN-TELLECTUALLY. BUT HE'S NOT PRETENTIOUS OR POMPOUS IN ANY WAY. HE'S VERY APPROACHABLE."

— *Dylan Gandy*, *former Texas Tech center*

"COACH LEACH IS WHAT I'D CALL A 'PLAIN JANE' COMPETITIVE COACH. HE DOESN'T ACCEPT ANYTHING LESS THAN THE BEST. IF WE'RE NOT RUNNING IT RIGHT, HE DOESN'T CARE IF WE'RE THERE UNTIL NINE AT NIGHT. HE JUST HAS A LOT OF FIRE AND IS VERY EX-CITED ABOUT BEING HERE."

— *Tim Baker*, *Texas Tech wide receiver, on Leach, 2000*

"HE IS A GREAT PLAYERS' COACH. I THINK HE HAS COME A LONG WAYS. I LOVE SITTING DOWN AND TALKING TO HIM IN PRACTICE IN SPARE TIMES. WE DO SPRING DRILLS WHERE COACH LEACH STOPS AND THINKS OF A NEW PLAY AND HE WILL THROW IT IN THE MIDDLE. HE IS A LOT OF FUN."

— *E. J. Whitley, Texas Tech offensive tackle*

"I'D CALL HIM A CHARACTER. HE'S VERY INTELLIGENT. HE CAN BE SILLY AT TIMES, BUT HE'S A GOOD GUY."

— *Joel Filani, Texas Tech wide receiver, on Leach*

"HE'S A DIFFERENT TYPE OF COACH, VERY UNIQUE. HE'S A VERY LAID-BACK GUY ACTUALLY AND EASY TO PLAY FOR."

— *Cody Hodges*

"I'M INTRIGUED WITH HOW HE DOES WHAT HE DOES. IT SEEMS SIMPLE AS HE CALLS HIS PLAYS AND SIPS COFFEE. BUT I THINK REALLY WHERE HIS GENIUS LIES IS IN HIS RELATIONSHIPS WITH HIS PLAYERS. PUBLICLY, WE GET THE SENSE HE'S CHALLENGING, CALLING THEM OUT, CALLING THEM NAMES. BUT I THINK HE'S EARNED THE RIGHT TO DO THAT PUBLICLY BECAUSE HE'S EARNED THEIR TRUST PRIVATELY. I THINK THEY REALLY ADMIRE HIM. I HAD SOME GUYS WHEN I WAS WITH THE BALTIMORE RAVENS (SUCH AS LINEBACKER MIKE SMITH) THAT ABSOLUTELY LOVED HIM."

— *Rick Neuheisel, on Leach's offense and players*

"THE THING IS, HE'S PROBABLY ONE OF THE FUNNIER GUYS YOU'LL EVER TALK TO. HE KNOWS ANYTHING ABOUT EVERYTHING. YOU NAME IT, WESTERN MOVIES, PIRATE STUFF . . . JUST WEIRD STUFF YOU'D NEVER THINK A FOOTBALL COACH WOULD THINK ABOUT. HE HAS NO SENSE OF TIME. HE JUST KIND OF GOES ABOUT IT, THEN HE'LL LOOK AT THE CLOCK AND GO, 'OH, MAN, IT'S THAT LATE? BETTER GO ON TO THE NEXT THING.'

"HE IS A DIFFERENT GUY, BUT I THINK HE ENJOYS BEING DIFFERENT. HIS BEING DIFFERENT HAS MADE HIM SO SUCCESSFUL."

— **Wes Welker**

"HE TELLS A LOT OF JOKES AND TELLS A LOT OF STORIES. SOMETIMES, PEOPLE HAVE TROUBLE FOLLOWING HIS STORIES, ACTUALLY."

— **Cody Lloyd**, *Texas Tech wide receiver*

"HE'S ONE OF THOSE GUYS WHO TELLS A JOKE THAT ONLY HE GETS, YOU KNOW. SOMETIMES HE'S ALL BUSINESS; HE'S JUST A DIFFERENT BREED OF PERSON."

— **Adell Duckett**, *Texas Tech defensive lineman*

"COACH'S MOTIVATIONAL SPEECHES ARE ALWAYS THE SAME. HE TELLS VERY LONG STORIES, AND YOU'RE NEVER SURE WHAT THEY MEAN, BUT HE'S A GENIUS. WHEN WE LEAVE THE LOCKER ROOM, WE ALL KNOW THAT WE'LL HAVE THREE RECEIVERS WIDE OPEN EVERY PLAY."

— **Daniel Loper**, *Texas Tech offensive lineman*

"HE'S ONE OF THOSE GUYS WHO, WHEN HE SAYS SOMETHING, HE SAYS IT IN A DIFFERENT WAY. HE THINKS OUTSIDE THE BOX, AND IT'S A REALLY SMART BOX. . . . LAST YEAR, AFTER THE TEXAS GAME (A 59-43 LOSS), HE STARTED TALKING ABOUT HOW THE CHICKEN WAS INVOLVED BUT THE PIG WAS COMMITTED. IT WAS SOME KIND OF HAM AND EGG ANALOGY."

— Darcel McBath, Texas Tech safety

"THEY'RE ALL JUST REALLY GOOD GUYS. ESPECIALLY COACH LEACH. MY PARENTS REALLY LIKE HIM, AND SO DO I. HE'S JUST A GENUINE GUY. I MEAN, WHEN YOU THINK OF HEAD FOOTBALL COACHES, YOU THINK OF THESE GUYS WHO MIGHT THINK THEY'RE PRETTY COOL AND STUFF, BUT NOT COACH LEACH. HE'S NOT A POLITICIAN LIKE, SAY, MACK BROWN OR SOMEONE. HE'S JUST REALLY DOWN-TO-EARTH AND VERY HONEST."

— Taylor Charbonnet, Texas Tech recruit,
on Leach and the Texas Tech coaching staff

"HE'S DISHEVELED, TENDS TO MUMBLE, AND TALKS IN CIRCLES THAT ONLY ADD TO HIS MYSTERY."

— Scott Pelley, CBS-TV 60 Minutes reporter

"WHEN I MET HIM (LEACH), HE WAS THIS DUDE IN THE CORNER WITH MESSY HAIR AND WEARING SWEATS. I THOUGHT IF HE CAN COACH, I OUGHT TO GET IN THE PROFESSION."

— Dana Holgorsen, West Virginia coach,
recalling meeting Leach for the first time

"HE'S A PRETTY ECLECTIC GUY. HE'S GOING TO DO SOME THINGS OTHER COACHES ARE NOT GOING TO DO. YOU GET HIM TALKING ABOUT OFFENSE, HE'LL SAY IT'S A TOOL FOR THE PLAYERS TO DO THEIR JOB, IT'S KIND OF LIKE BEING A PIRATE USING A SWORD. ANOTHER ONE HE'S BIG ON IS GERONIMO AND THE INDIANS. WHEN WE WERE AT VALDOSTA STATE, ALL OF THE PLAYERS LOVED HIM BECAUSE THEY'D GO BY HIS OFFICE AND SOMETIMES HE WAS SO CAPTIVATING TALKING ABOUT HISTORICAL STUFF THAT I HAD GUYS MISS CLASS BE-CAUSE THEY'D BE LISTENING TO LEACH LECTURE ABOUT GERONIMO."

— *Hal Mumme*, *McMurry coach, who hired an at-the-time un-known Leach at Iowa Wesleyan, Valdosta State, and Kentucky*

"FOR THIRTY MINUTES, HE WAS TELLING ME ABOUT HOW I SHOULD STAY. THE OTHER HALF, I DON'T EVEN REMEMBER. THERE WAS SOME PIRATES, SOME SKI TRIPS COMING UP."

— *Michael Crabtree*, *Texas Tech wide receiver, recalling a conversation in which Leach urged him to stay in school instead of going to the NFL*

"I'M AMAZED BY HIM. HE'S LIKE A MAD SCIENTIST, AND I DON'T MEAN THAT IN A DEROGATORY FASHION. HE'S NOT AFRAID TO TRY ANY-THING, AND HE HAS A SUCCESS RATE THAT AMAZES ME. HE'S ECCEN-TRIC, AND I'M NOT SURE HE WORKS AT IT. HE IS WHAT HE IS, AND THAT'S THE WAY IT IS."

— *Spike Dykes*, *former Texas Tech coach*

"HIS STRATEGY IS GOOD, HIS SCHEME IS GOOD, BUT WHAT MAKES HIM A GENIUS IS HIS BELIEF AND CONFIDENCE IN IT. THE PLAYERS HAVE TAKEN ON THE PERSONALITY OF COACH LEACH. THEY BELIEVE STRONGLY IN WHAT THEY DO."

— *Sonny Cumbie*, *former Texas Tech quarterback*

"HE'S A GREAT COACH AND A REALLY SMART GUY WHO KNOWS WHAT HE'S TALKING ABOUT. I COMPLETELY AGREE WITH THOSE WHO SAY HE'S A BIT QUIRKY, BUT AT THE SAME TIME, YOU EITHER LOVE HIM OR HATE HIM. HE'S THE KIND OF COACH WHO'S NOT SUPER TALKATIVE, BUT HE CAN TALK TO YOU ABOUT ALL KINDS OF THINGS LIKE HISTORY AND THE JFK ASSASSINATION. HE IS A PRETTY INTERESTING GUY."

— *Tyler Yenzer, former Texas Tech defensive end*

"I DON'T HAVE MUCH TO COMPARE IT TO. IT'S FUN TO WIN, AND COACH LEACH IS A WINNER. IT'S FUN, EXCITING TO PLAY FOR A COACH WHO HAS A PASSION FOR THE GAME. HE LIKES THINGS TO BE DONE PERFECT. SOMETIMES, YOU'RE LIKE, 'THIS DOESN'T MAKE ANY SENSE,' BUT THEN LATER, YOU'LL LOOK BACK AND SAY, 'YEAH, THAT MADE SENSE.' IT'S THE LITTLE THINGS . . . IT ALL MAKES SENSE. THERE IS A METHOD TO HIS MADNESS, EVEN WHEN IT SOMETIMES DOES JUST SEEM LIKE CRAZINESS. THERE'S ALWAYS A REASON."

— *Baron Batch, Texas Tech running back, when asked to describe what it's like to play for Leach*

"IT'S DIFFERENT, BUT HE MEANS WELL. HE DOESN'T SAY ANYTHING TO YOU WITHOUT A PURPOSE. EVERYTHING HAS A MEANING. HE JUST COMES OFF AS A DIFFERENT TYPE OF PERSON, SO IT TAKES SOMEBODY TO BE AROUND HIM MORE TO UNDERSTAND WHAT TYPE OF PERSON HE IS."

— *Vince Mayle, Washington State receiver, when asked what it's like to be around and coached by Leach*

"MIKE LEACH IS AN OLD SCHOOL COACH. HE BELIEVES IN DISCIPLINE. IF YOU DON'T DO IT RIGHT, YOU ARE GOING TO PAY FOR IT. I WAS USED TO THAT TYPE OF COACHING IN HIGH SCHOOL. HE WOULD GET IN YOUR FACE. HE GOT ME IN A GOOD MINDSET. IT IS MORE MENTAL THAN PHYSICAL. I APPRECIATE ALL OF THE LIFE LESSONS THAT MIKE LEACH GAVE US."

— *Xavier Cooper, former Washington State defensive tackle*

"HE PUSHED HIS PLAYERS AND COACHES AS HARD AS ANYBODY I HAVE EVER BEEN AROUND, BUT HE IS FAIR TO EVERY PLAYER."

— *Graham Harrell, former Texas Tech quarterback*

"I DON'T CARE IF YOU'RE AN ALL-AMERICAN OR A WALK-ON, HE'LL TREAT YOU THE SAME."

— *Daniel Loper, former Texas Tech offensive lineman*

"I THINK THIS CHANGE IS LONG OVERDUE. WE GOT A REAL TASK. MIKE DOESN'T WAVER. HE IS NOT WISHY-WASHY."

— *Bill Moos, Washington State athletic director,
on Leach's holding players accountable for
their performance while rebuilding the program*

"IT MIGHT TAKE YOU A LITTLE WHILE TO GET USED TO COACH LEACH."

— *Travis Long, Washington State linebacker*

"HE NEVER PLAYED COLLEGE FOOTBALL, BUT THE PLAYERS REALLY RELATE TO HIM BECAUSE HE'S JUST KIND OF AN EASY GUY TO GET ALONG WITH. AND HE HAS A UNIQUE WAY OF CALLING PEOPLE OUT WHEN THEY MESS UP, WHERE THEY DON'T TAKE IT PERSONALLY."

— **Dusty Bonner**, *former Kentucky quarterback*

"HE MAKES IT FUN AND ALLOWS THE PLAYERS TO HAVE A GOOD TIME AND TO BE THEMSELVES. YOU CAN SMILE AROUND HERE. HE PROVES YOU CAN WIN WITHOUT MAKING EVERYBODY MISERABLE. BUT IT'S FOOTBALL, NOT ALL RAINBOWS AND PUPPY DOGS. HE'S GOING TO DEMAND YOU DO THINGS THE RIGHT WAY AND DO THEM WITH TREMENDOUS EFFORT."

— **Sonny Dykes**, *Texas Tech assistant coach*

"HE IS ECCENTRIC. HE MAYBE THINKS WITH A DIFFERENT SIDE OF HIS BRAIN THAN MOST PEOPLE DO, BUT HIS METHODS ARE EFFECTIVE."

— **Guy Morriss**, *Baylor coach, who coached with Leach at Kentucky*

"HE IS UNBELIEVABLY ENTERTAINING. BUT HE IS EXCEPTIONALLY INTELLIGENT, AND HE KNOWS EXACTLY HOW HE IS COMING ACROSS. IT'S CALCULATED. HE MIGHT SAY SOMETHING OFF THE WALL OR OUTSIDE THE BOX, BUT HE KNOWS EVERYTHING THAT IS GOING ON. HE IS AN EXTREMELY CEREBRAL GUY."

— **Kyle Whittingham**, *Utah coach*

"NOW, THERE'S NO QUESTION MIKE IS AN ODD DUCK. BUT I'VE GOT A MATH DEPARTMENT FULL OF UNUSUAL PERSONALITIES. IT'S A COLLEGE CAMPUS. YOU'RE GOING TO HAVE SOME UNUSUAL PERSONALITIES."

— **Guy Bailey**, *Tech president, shortly after Leach was fired, 2010*

"HE'S GOT A LOT OF THOUGHTS. HE'S GOT A LOT ON HIS MIND. HE'S A MULTITASKER, TO SAY THE LEAST. HE'S A MULTI-CONVERSATIONALIST."

— **Brent Venables**, *defensive coordinator at Oklahoma when Leach was on the staff there*

"YOU'VE GOT TO REMEMBER HE'S FROM CODY, WYOMING, WHICH IS A RODEO TOWN UP BY YELLOWSTONE. HE'S GOT THAT OLD WESTERN DEAL. HE'S A STORYTELLER. WE'LL SIT AROUND JUST TALKING, AND THE NEXT THING YOU KNOW, IT'S FOUR HOURS LATER. HE'S JUST VERY, VERY BRIGHT."

— **Manny Matsakis**, *Texas Tech assistant coach, 2001*

"HERE'S A GUY THAT CAN TALK TO YOU ABOUT THE EUROPEAN UNION AND HOWARD STERN IN ONE CONVERSATION. HE'S THAT DI-VERSE."

— **Mark Mangino**, *Kansas coach, who coached with Leach at Oklahoma*

"I guess it's good to evolve, kind of evolutionary, you know. so that's good evolvement. Tell him I think he's evolved, too."

— **Leach**, *when told Kansas Coach Mark Mangino said Leach has done a good job evolving through the years*

"YOU CAN GET INTO A CONVERSATION WITH LEACH ON COVER 2 AND END UP ON NORWEGIAN BLUEBERRIES."

— **Trevor Reilly**, *Utah defensive end, who was recruited by Leach when the coach was at Texas Tech*

"WHEN SPIKE WAS AT TEXAS TECH . . . I THOUGHT HE DID THE BEST JOB ANYBODY COULD DO AT TECH. IT HAD HIS PERSONALITY. THEN MIKE CAME IN — HE WASN'T FROM THAT PART OF THE COUNTRY. HE WAS GOING TO THROW THE BALL ALL THE TIME INTO THAT BIG WIND AND NOBODY THOUGHT HE COULD DO IT. GIVE HIM CREDIT. HE HAS TAKEN HIS PERSONALITY AND HIS OFFENSE AND HE HAS DONE EX-ACTLY WHAT HE HAS WANTED TO DO WITH IT. . . . I AM AMAZED AT THE THINGS HE HAS ACCOMPLISHED."

*— **Mack Brown**, University of Texas coach, 2005*

"HE'S THE COLUMBO OF FOOTBALL COACHING. THAT'S WHAT HE IS. DUMB LIKE A FOX AND SMARTER THAN MOST. BELIEVE ME, HE KNOWS EXACTLY WHAT HE'S DOING. HE SUCKS A LOT OF US RIGHT IN THERE. LET ME TELL YOU THAT."

*— **Glen Mason**, University of Minnesota coach*

"MIKE LEACH IS LIKE A FOX. SOME COACHES GO OUT AND THEY HOB-NOB WITH THE BOOSTERS AND SO FORTH. MIKE HOBNOBS WITH HIM-SELF AND HIS WIFE, SHARON. HE DOES ALL THAT CRAZY PIRATE STUFF AND ALL THOSE CRAZY THINGS. THE GUY IS REALLY SHARP THE WAY HE DOES STUFF."

*— **Gil Brandt,** former Dallas Cowboys executive*
and long-time college football talent-evaluation expert

"MIKE'S A FUN COACH TO WATCH WORK, BECAUSE HE'S A CONTRAR-IAN. HE'S DIFFERENT THAN A LOT OF COACHES. HE'S GOT A LOT OF GREAT IDEAS. I'M SURE THAT HIS BACKGROUND WITH HAL MUMME HAS A LOT TO DO WITH THAT, BUT HE'S FUN TO WATCH."

*— **Terry Donahue**, broadcaster/former coach*

"DON'T EVER PLAY TRIVIAL PURSUIT WITH MIKE BECAUSE YOU'LL LOSE. HE HAS AN EXTREMELY QUICK MIND. HE TALKS SLOW, BUT HIS MIND HAS A WEALTH OF FACTS."

— *Frank Leach*, *Mike's father*

"I was a kid who actually used the encyclopedia."

— *Leach*

"WE WERE ALL RAISED BY MIKE. IN A SENSE, WE GREW UP WITH HIM. LIKE LINCOLN (RILEY), LIKE DANA (HOLGORSEN), LIKE SONNY (CUMBIE), OR OTHERS, I WAS ONE OF THOSE GUYS WHO HAD AN OPPORTUNITY TO SIT THERE AND LEARN THE GOOD FROM MIKE AND PUT MY OWN SPIN ON IT."

— *Dennis Simmons*, *longtime Leach assistant,*
after leaving Washington State for a job at Oklahoma

"I'M FOREVER GRATEFUL TO MIKE LEACH. THERE'S NOT MANY GUYS WHO WOULD BELIEVE IN SOMEBODY AND HIRE A YOUNG COACH AT A BIG-TIME UNIVERSITY. HE NEVER BLINKED AN EYE. HE TAUGHT ME A LOT. OFFENSIVELY, HE KNEW EXACTLY WHAT HE WANTED TO DO. AND MOST IMPORTANTLY, THERE WAS NO DOUBT IN HIS MIND. HE BELIEVED, 100 PERCENT, THAT WE WERE THE BEST ON THE FIELD. AND THAT'S SOMETHING I'VE CARRIED OVER TO EVERY PLACE I'VE BEEN."

— *Seth Littrell*, *on being named head coach at the University*
of North Texas. The former Oklahoma running back was twenty-
five when Leach hired him as running backs coach at Texas Tech.

"MIKE GAVE ME MY FIRST SHOT, HIRED ME AT TEXAS TECH WHEN I WAS TWENTY-THREE, BELIEVED IN ME WHEN A LOT OF PEOPLE TOLD HIM HE SHOULDN'T. WE ALL HAVE THAT COACH, THAT PERSON THAT GAVE US THAT FIRST BREAK. HE WAS THAT FOR ME, AND I'LL NEVER FORGET HIM FOR THAT."

— *Lincoln Riley, University of Oklahoma offensive coordinator and a former Leach assistant at Texas Tech*

"MIKE LEACH IS UNLIKE EVERY COACH IN THE HISTORY OF COLLEGE FOOTBALL. IT OPENED UP MY EYES TO DOING THINGS IN TERMS OF COACHING AND A DIFFERENT WAY OF MOTIVATING PLAYERS, TO BE HONEST. I STILL CARRY OVER A LOT OF THOSE LESSONS."

— *Kliff Kingsbury, Texas Tech head coach, who was Leach's first quarterback at Tech*

"I DON'T KNOW WHO THIS GUY IS, AND I DON'T CARE IF HE GOES ON TO BIG WINS AND BIG SEASONS. I DON'T WANT TO BE AROUND SOMEONE WHO TREATS PEOPLE THIS WAY. I CAN'T SORT OUT BEING A COUGAR AND BEING AROUND THIS GUY. I'M PROUD OF THE COUGAR WAY AND HOW COUGARS OPERATE AND THE CULTURE OF WHICH THEY ARE. HE'S EMBARRASSING MY PROFESSION. HE'S TAKING ME SOMEWHERE I DON'T WANT TO GO. . . . I SAID SINCE DAY ONE (WHEN LEACH WAS HIRED) THAT IT WOULD SET US BACK, AND THAT WAS BEFORE I FOUND OUT WHAT A WEIRD DUDE HE WAS. I'VE BEEN UPSET SINCE LAST DECEMBER, AND I DON'T SEE MYSELF FEELING ANY BETTER FOR A WHILE."

— *Jim Walden, former Washington State coach, 2012*

The Mike Leach coaching tree includes current college head coaches Dana Holgersen (West Virginia), Kliff Kingsbury (Texas Tech), Seth Littrell (University of North Texas), and Sonny Dykes (California).

"WHEN I FIRST MET HIM, I THOUGHT, 'IS THIS GUY REALLY THE HEAD COACH? THIS CAN'T BE REAL.'"

> — ***Graham Harrell***, *former Tech quarterback, on meeting Leach*

"WHEN YOU FIRST MEET HIM, YOU THINK HE'S AN EQUIPMENT MANAGER."

> — ***Jarrett Hicks***, *Texas Tech wide receiver*

"You draw on Scouting. It sets a code for your life. Imagine how screwed up I'd be without that."

> — ***Leach***, *a former Eagle Scout*

17
Lubbock in My Rearview Mirror (Chancellors, Presidents, and Contracts)

"If it's controversial to have the highest graduation rate in the country and to go to ten straight bowls and to improve every year and win a bunch of bowl games and not have your players get in trouble and not get NCAA violations, then I'm controversial. I'll just have to live with it."

— **Leach**, reflecting on his success and
controversial firing at Texas Tech in 2009

By any account, Mike Leach's dismissal from Texas Tech in December 2009 was very bitter, very nasty, and very public.

An alumni and fan base was left divided as the school's all-time-winningest coach was terminated for allegedly mistreating (never proven) a player (Adam James), whose father (Craig James) happened to work for a national TV sports network (ESPN). "Insubordination" was another reason cited for the coach's forced departure.

Ultimately, nobody was a winner, with Tech taking a huge national PR hit, while suffering the wrath of alumni and fans; Leach being left without a coaching job for two years; and the elder James leaving ESPN for a dismal run for public office.

But how did it all reach that point of no return?

Lubbock was not quite sure what to think of Mike Leach when he came to town in 2000 with his newfangled, pass-first, run-second offense. And, on a personal level, he was certainly no "good old boy" like

Spike Dykes, who masterfully worked the Bubbas as well as the regents, boosters, and alums on the country club circuit. Leach, the outsider, preferred such pursuits as rollerblading and movies, as opposed to golf and formal banquets, and wasn't particularly comfortable mingling and schmoozing. The laid-back Leach favored shorts/jeans and sandals/flip-flops to the corporate business suit attire favored by some coaches.

It quickly became apparent that the Lubbock "establishment" had a difficult time accepting the fact that Mike Leach was different. That Mike Leach was Mike Leach and not Spike Dykes or Steve Sloan or J. T. King, for that matter.

It didn't help that his first two seasons resulted in Spike-like records of 7-6 and 7-5, while the Air Raid offense was still evolving.

Early on, Leach and athletic director/old school basketball coach Gerald Myers clashed on scheduling, summer camps, and budgeting issues, with words of discontent leaking out to the media at various times.

The "establishment's" reluctance to embrace Leach and the disconnect between the two was perhaps best voiced in a series of frank columns by a well-respected and longtime journalist at the *Lubbock Avalanche-Journal*.

After Tech opened the 2002 season with a lopsided loss at Ohio State, the writer penned a mean-spirited column about Leach. One could only assume that the opinion reflected that of the "establishment" in Lubbock.

Titled, "Leach needs a new strategy, both on the field and off," the column read, in part:

"Football season is only one game old and I'm already sick of Mike Leach. . . . In my opinion, Tech did wind up with a jerk among its head coaches and, to the delightful surprise of many, it ain't Bobby Knight. . . . Leach, due to his seemingly reclusive ways and reluctance to engage in community activities, has never endeared himself to Lubbock's citizenry, certainly not to the extent that Spike did."

The writer then went on to criticize the effectiveness of Leach's unique (at the time) pass-happy offense.

Keep in mind that this was written two seasons (plus one game) into the Leach era, a time in which the coach had posted a record of 14-12.

Fast forward now to November 30, 2008, and another column by the same writer appeared, bearing this headline: "Sometimes a guy has to admit he was wrong and apologize."

This time, he wrote, in part: "Back in early September six years ago, I wrote a piece in which I took Mike Leach to task over his coaching strategy and his very personality. That I prejudged the former and misjudged the latter is what put me in a position of having to write a piece that I know will miss the mark of atonement but hopefully will accomplish its main purpose — saying on the record that I was dead wrong about Leach . . . the man, the coach . . . Mike Leach, as it turns out, is a genius."

The columnist went on to write that, "It doesn't make it any easier that, at the time that I wrote the earlier piece, I was not alone in my assessment." Then he adds this revelation, which one would assume the Tech administration would rather have been kept quiet, especially in light of later legal action:

"Not only did the majority of the heavy run of mail generated by that column agree with the commentary, even Mike's bosses at Tech were privately hoping that he'd soon find work on some other campus."

It should be noted that between the columns of August 31, 2002, and November 30, 2008, Leach had suddenly become a coaching "genius," compiling a record of 61-26 during that time, with his record-breaking offense bringing the team and university unprecedented national recognition. As noted in the second column, Tech actually rose to the number-two ranking in the nation in 2008 before a one-sided loss to Oklahoma.

Coincidentally, between the timing of the columns, Tech notched such triumphs as a 70-10 pasting of Nebraska in 2004 and a come-from-behind 44-41 decision over Minnesota in the 2006 Insight

Bowl. Tech had trailed Minnesota 35-7 at the half, 38-7 in the third quarter, and then rallied to post the biggest comeback in bowl game history.

In fairness, the writer also mentions in his "apology" column that he may be accused of jumping on the bandwagon.

He concludes: "But, getting back to the original topic: Do I now regret having written that column all those years and offensive yards ago?

"Yes, I do. I'm sorry I did it.

"I also envy those of you who knew right from the start that Mike Leach was the real deal.

"There's sure a lot more of you today than there was back then . . . "

Meanwhile, success on the football field didn't necessarily translate into peace off the field between the coach and the administration.

Following a successful 9-4 season in 2007, Leach was looking to renegotiate his contract to bring it more in line with his Big 12 peers. The coach and his agents thought they had an agreement in place, but Tech officials balked, and, instead, delayed the contract talks until after the 2008 season.

Having piloted the Red Raiders to an 11-2 mark in 2008, Leach seemingly held the upper hand as the contract talks were renewed.

What turned into an extremely contentious negotiation involving agents, presidents, chancellors, regents, and even former regents, finally ended successfully when Leach and chancellor Kent Hance sat down and agreed on a three-year extension on a five-year, $12.7 million contract. Included was an $800,000 completion bonus that Leach would receive on December 31, 2009, if he were still the coach.

Throughout the negotiation process, both sides expressed animosity: Leach believed he was underpaid and didn't appreciate some of the clauses the University added to the proposed contract; the University didn't appreciate Leach's agents' interference, public posturing, and the coach's apparent flirtatious desire to seek employment elsewhere.

Leach might have won the contract battle in February 2009, but he lost the war. Ten months later, after the Adam James situation, Leach was fired. And coincidentally(?), he was terminated on December 30, 2009, precisely one day before he was due the $800,000 completion bonus.

"SOURCES TELL ME MIKE LEACH IS EXPERIENCING PROBLEMS IN HIS FIRST SEASON AS HEAD COACH OF TEXAS TECH. REPORTEDLY, LEACH AND HIS PRESIDENT (DAVID SCHMIDLY) HAVEN'T BEEN SEEING EYE TO EYE. HARD AS IT MAY SEEM TO BELIEVE, IT MAY BE OVER FOR LEACH AFTER JUST ONE YEAR."

— *Dave Baker*, The Cats' Pause, *2000*

"MY THEORY IS THAT THERE IS AN ORCHESTRATED ATTEMPT, PROBABLY ASSOCIATED WITH RECRUITING (TO MALIGN LEACH). MIKE IS BRINGING IN SOME STUD ATHLETES, AND HE'S BRINGING THEM IN FROM ALL OVER THE COUNTRY. I THINK HE'S RIPPING INTO (OTHER) PEOPLE'S RECRUITING, AND I THINK WE'VE GOT PEOPLE TRYING TO DO MIKE IN BECAUSE OF IT. . . . I THINK MIKE AND HIS STAFF HAVE DONE A TERRIFIC JOB. HOW ANYBODY IN THE WORLD COULD CONSTRUE TRASH LIKE THIS IS UNBELIEVABLE TO ME."

— *David Schmidly*, Texas Tech president, on a published
report out of Lexington, Kentucky, that he and first-year
coach Leach didn't get along and that a coaching change
might be made. Leach threatened a libel suit and
later received a retraction-clarification from the publication, 2000

"I've never had a problem with this sort of thing. I want to make it clear that if anybody prints falsehoods about me, the team, or the University, there is going to be a price to pay. Then I want to prove that all allegations are false."

— *Leach*

"MIKE LEACH HAS DONE A GREAT JOB FOR TEXAS TECH. HE HAS BROUGHT A COMMITMENT TO ESTABLISHING A NATIONAL PRESENCE FOR TEXAS TECH FOOTBALL. AT THE SAME TIME, HE HAS SET HIGH STANDARDS FOR HIS PLAYERS, NOT ONLY ON THE FOOTBALL FIELD, BUT ALSO IN THE CLASSROOM. WE LOOK FORWARD TO A CONTINUED RELATIONSHIP WITH MIKE AND HIS STAFF."

*— **Schmidly**, announcing a contract extension for Leach, 2000*

"I WAS IN MAJOR LEAGUE POLITICS FOR TWENTY YEARS, AND THE NASTINESS OF THAT DOESN'T HOLD A CANDLE TO THIS RECRUITING AND RUMOR BUSINESS. THE EVIDENCE IS PRETTY SOLID THAT THE IN-TERNET RUMORS WERE COMING FROM ADVOCATES OF OTHER SCHOOLS AND WE NEEDED TO PUT A STOP TO IT. THAT'S ONE OF THE REASONS (FOR THE CONTRACT EXTENSION)."

*— **John T. Montford**, Texas Tech chancellor, 2000*

"It's great news. It just reaffirms the commitment the school has to me and to building a great program. The support from the administration has been unwavering from the get-go, and it's very much appreciated. It's the only school I've ever been around where the chancellor and the president come out to practice at least once or twice a week. There's just a big commitment to football."

*— **Leach**, after Tech rewarded the coach with an extension of his original five-year contract and referring to Chancellor John T. Montford and President David Schmidly, 2000*

"WE HAD SOME COMMUNICATION PROBLEMS. IT WAS PROBABLY TRUER THAT MIKE WAS MORE UNHAPPY WITH US THAN VICE VERSA. WE HUDDLED UP AFTER THE N.C. STATE GAME AND TRIED TO ADDRESS HIS CONCERNS. I THINK WE'VE MOVED ON. WE RECOGNIZE WHAT MIKE HAS DONE, AND WE HOPE HE'LL CONTINUE AS OUR COACH."

— Schmidly, Texas Tech president, 2002

"STAMPS ARE NOT THE ISSUE. THE ISSUE IS WE NEED TO GENERATE MORE REVENUE TO HELP MIKE, BUT WE HAVE TO LIVE ON WHAT WE EARN. . . . THERE IS NOTHING THAT WOULD PLEASE ME MORE THAN TO GIVE MIKE LEACH MORE (BUDGET) MONEY. I MEAN NOTHING. BUT I DON'T HAVE A MINT ON THE CAMPUS, AND I CAN'T GIVE HIM MORE THAN WE MAKE. THAT'S THE ISSUE HERE."

— Schmidly, on controversy surrounding the fact that the football program had a budget deficit and the University stopped paying for the department's outgoing mail, 2002

"I HAVE NO PROBLEM WITH MIKE LEACH. HE'S A DAMN GOOD COACH."

— Schmidly, 2002

"I DON'T SAY 'I' A LOT. BUT I WANT MIKE TO BE OUR COACH. WE'RE GOING TO WORK TO THAT END TO KEEP HIM AS OUR COACH. . . . I LIKE THE WAY OUR TEAM IS GOING AND THE WAY THIS PROGRAM IS GOING. I THINK HE'S DOING A GREAT JOB WITH OUR TEAM."

— Gerald Myers, Texas Tech athletic director, on working on a contract extension and raise for Leach, 2003

"I THINK YOU CAN SAFELY SAY THAT OUR FOOTBALL COACH WILL BE PAID COMPARABLE TO THE MARKET OF BIG 12 COACHES."

— Myers, 2003

"I've specifically concentrated on not concentrating on this, and up to this point, I've done a really good job. This is a great deal, great situation, great everything. I love it here, and I want to stay here and all the rest."

— Leach, on his agents and Tech working
on a new contract during the 2003 season

"BY ABOUT THE THIRD YEAR (2002), FANS SAW HOW EXCITING THIS STYLE OF FOOTBALL CAN BE. PLUS, I THINK MIKE HAS MATURED AND GROWN AS A HEAD COACH AS WELL. I THINK HE WASN'T REAL INTERESTED IN THE (PUBLIC SPEAKING) PART OF IT, BUT MIKE HAS IMPROVED A LOT IN THAT AREA. HE'S GOT A GOOD SENSE OF HUMOR. I DON'T THINK THAT CAME THROUGH THE FIRST COUPLE OF YEARS LIKE IT DOES NOW."

—Myers

"As a head coach, you're on two lists. You're the guy that might get fired, or you're the guy who might go somewhere. Given the two lists, I guess that's the one to be on."

— Leach, when asked about periodically being mentioned as
a candidate for various college head-coaching vacancies, 2004

"I think Chancellor (David) Smith has done a tremendous job here. As the keystone person of the university, I think he's done some great things. I think Texas Tech is headed in the right direction, and he's one of the big reasons why."

— Leach, 2004

"WE'RE PLEASED WITH THE DIRECTION OUR FOOTBALL TEAM HAS BEEN GOING THE LAST FEW YEARS AND THE JOB THAT MIKE AND HIS STAFF HAVE DONE. WE WANT MIKE TO BE OUR COACH, AND WE WANT HIM TO BE IN THAT POSITION A LONG TIME."

— Myers, 2005

"I mean it's an interesting question. I've been there nine years, which is longer than most marriages or jobs, you know."

— Leach, when asked if he wanted to remain at Tech, 2008

"I THINK THAT THIS IS THE BEST JOB THAT (LEACH) IS GOING TO GET. MIKE'S A LITTLE DIFFERENT, BUT WE LIKE MIKE OUT HERE. HE'D PROBABLY HAVE A MORE DIFFICULT TIME AT SOME OTHER PLACE WHERE HE HAS TO PLAY GOLF WITH BOOSTERS AND STUFF. WE JUST WANT MIKE TO COACH FOOTBALL OUT HERE AND TELL PIRATE STORIES."

— Kent Hance, Texas Tech chancellor

"WE ARE DEFINITELY GOING TO KEEP MIKE LEACH. HE'S A GREAT COACH, HE'S A GREAT GUY, AND HE'S GOING TO GET A NEW CONTRACT AT THE END OF THE SEASON. WE ARE PROUD OF HIM AND WE'RE LOOKING FORWARD TO HIS NEXT VICTORIES. I DON'T WANT TO DISTRACT OR DO ANYTHING TO DISTRACT HIM FROM TAKING CARE OF BUSINESS. WE ARE GOING TO TAKE CARE OF EVERYTHING,

AND MIKE LEACH IS GOING TO BE THE COACH AT TEXAS TECH FOR A LONG TIME."

—Hance, on not re-signing Leach to a new contract in the midst of a successful season, 2008

"WE'RE GOING TO GET THAT DONE WHEN THE SEASON'S OVER. IT'S NOT EVEN A QUESTION THAT WE WANT MIKE. WE DO WANT HIM. WE WANT TO HAVE MIKE DOWN HERE FOR A LONG TIME."

— Myers, on a contract extension, 2008

"THEY WANT TO WORK SOMETHING OUT, AND WE WANT TO WORK SOMETHING OUT. THIS ISN'T ABOUT MIKE LEACH. THIS IS A MONEY ISSUE. AND FOR ME, IT'S A QUESTION OF WHAT WE CAN AFFORD. WE DON'T HAVE AN UNLIMITED BUDGET. WE LIKE MIKE AND WE WANT TO KEEP HIM, BUT WE HAVE TO USE GOOD SOUND JUDGMENT ALSO IN THE FINANCIAL STABILITY OF ALL OUR PROGRAMS."

— Hance, on talking to Leach's agents, December 2008

"It's well documented that we want to be at Texas Tech for years to come. Our results have been positive, and I have no regrets whatsoever. We're very excited about the future of the program. We had a strong recruiting class. We've won more bowl games and had the best season in the history of Texas Tech. I'm trying to focus on my job."

— Leach, during the negotiations

"I LIKE MIKE AND I WANT HIM TO BE OUR COACH, BUT I DON'T WANT HIS AGENTS SHOPPING HIM AROUND EVERY YEAR. I FOUND IT OUT-RAGEOUS THAT I SAW IN THE NEWSPAPER MY FOOTBALL COACH WAS INTERVIEWING FOR OTHER JOBS. WE EXPECT HIM TO NOTIFY US. WE WANT LOYALTY. . . . IF IT'S GOOD FOR ONE, IT'S GOOD FOR THE OTHER. HIS AGENTS SAY MACK BROWN AND BOB STOOPS DON'T HAVE A BUY-OUT PROVISION, AND I TOLD THEM WHEN MIKE WINS A NATIONAL CHAMPIONSHIP, I'LL TAKE THE BUYOUT PROVISION OUT."

> — *Hance*, *on the guarantee and buyout clauses added to Leach's proposed contract, February 2009*

"I don't have to have hall passes on this one."

> — *Leach, objecting to a provision in his proposed contract that would trigger his firing and a $1.5 million penalty if he interviewed for another job without athletic director Gerald Myers's permission.*

"COACH LEACH HAS DECLINED OUR $12.7 MILLION CONTRACT. WE WILL ENTER THE DECISION-MAKING PROCESS AND SHOULD HAVE SOME ANNOUNCEMENTS BY NEXT WEEK. OUR DECISIONS WILL BE BASED ON THE BEST INTEREST OF TEXAS TECH AND ALL OF ITS SUP-PORTERS."

> — *Myers*

"I am prepared to finish out the last two years of my contract. I am not familiar with the notion of firing someone for failing to sign an extension to a contract. That notion to me is mind-numbing. But I guess stranger things have happened. I don't know what part of this is based in rumor or fact, but I can't fathom it. Maybe there are reasons I don't know about."

— **Leach**, *after rejecting the Tech contract offer and referring to the school's board of regents scheduling a teleconference to discuss "consideration of matters addressed by Section 02.03.2, Regents' Rules — including but not limited to the position of the football head coach."*

"I've always felt like it's good. I haven't had cross words with them. But by the same token, as far as their business and what's going on with this thing (contract), I have folks (agents) who handle it."

— **Leach**, *on his relationship with the Tech administration*

"I RESPECT MIKE AND ALL THAT HE'S DONE FOR TEXAS TECH FOOTBALL. THANKS TO HIM WE HAVE SOLD-OUT GAMES AND NATIONAL RANKINGS. WE'RE VERY PROUD OF MIKE. I'VE ALWAYS SAID THAT MIKE LEACH WAS A GREAT FIT FOR TEXAS TECH, AND I THINK HE FITS US WELL, AND WE LIKE HIM, AND WE LIKE FOR HIM TO BE HERE."

— **Hance**, *at a news conference announcing Leach's new contract, February 2009*

207

"TO PUT IT MILDLY, THIS HAS BEEN A TOUGH NEGOTIATION. IT'S BEEN A TOUGH TIME. IT'S REALLY GOOD TO GET IT BEHIND US. IT'S DONE AND WE'RE PLEASED. I KNOW A LOT OF YOU OUT THERE SAID WE WOULDN'T GET IT DONE. AND I WANT TO SAY THIS. I SAID THIS IN THE BEGINNING OF THE NEGOTIATIONS THAT I WANTED MIKE TO BE OUR COACH. I THINK THAT GOT LOST WITH ALL THE RHETORIC AND SPEC-ULATION AND EVERYTHING ELSE THROUGH THE PROCESS, BUT I'VE NEVER WAVERED ON THAT POINT. I WANTED HIM TO BE OUR COACH. I'M EXCITED ABOUT OUR FOOTBALL TEAM."

—Myers, at a news conference announcing Leach's new contract, February 2009

"Part of it was too many cooks in the kitchen. That's the biggest thing. Too many people get involved who don't need to be involved."

— Leach, on his contract negotiation difficulties, 2009

"I DON'T THINK THERE IS ANY BETTER PLACE FOR MIKE LEACH, AND HOPEFULLY, HE UNDERSTANDS THAT. I THINK HIS AGENT CREATED A LOT OF PROBLEMS AS FAR AS THAT SITUATION."

— Bob Knight, former Texas Tech basketball coach, on the contract difficulties

"Me and my family are thrilled to death that we're going to be in Lubbock for another five years. It's become a part of our family. At the rate that I get folks saying, 'Well, we just don't know if you like Lubbock.' I don't know how we could get rooted in here any deeper, so I've decided rather than messing with that, I'm going to say that I love Lubbock every single press conference."

> — **Leach**, *after signing a new contract*
> *amid speculation he wasn't happy in Lubbock*

"EARLY ON, PEOPLE THOUGHT HIS SUCCESS WAS A FLUKE. HE'S FINALLY GETTING THE CREDIT THAT HE SHOULD'VE GOTTEN FROM DAY ONE. WHAT MORE COULD YOU ASK IN TERMS OF PROVIDING EXCITEMENT, ENTERTAINMENT, AND GRADUATION RATES? HE'S BRINGING PLAYERS TO LUBBOCK THAT NEVER WOULD'VE COME THERE BEFORE. . . . WHATEVER REPORT CARD YOU WANT TO USE, HE GETS ALL A'S. I DON'T KNOW HOW MUCH BETTER HE COULD DO."

> — **John Scovell**, *Texas Tech board of regent (a former Red*
> *Raider quarterback), after Leach signed a new contract, 2009*

"I THINK WE MADE THE RIGHT DECISION. WE MADE THE RIGHT CHOICE. I THINK MIKE'S GROWN IN THIS JOB. HE WAS AN OFFENSIVE COORDINATOR THAT HAD GREAT UPSIDE, GREAT POTENTIAL AS A HEAD COACH. I THINK HE HAD AN IDEA ABOUT A LOT OF THINGS HE WANTED TO DO AS A HEAD COACH, BUT I THINK HE'S GOTTEN BETTER. I THINK HE'S GOTTEN BETTER EVERY YEAR."

> —**Myers**, *reflecting on the 1999 hiring of Leach, October 24, 2009*

"I THINK WE'VE HAD TIMES WE'VE HAD DISAGREEMENTS. BUT I'VE ALWAYS FELT STRONGLY THAT MIKE WAS DOING A GOOD JOB AND THAT PEOPLE ENJOYED TEXAS TECH FOOTBALL. I'VE ALWAYS REALIZED WHAT WE HAVE — THAT WE'RE AN ATTRACTIVE TEAM FOR TV AND THAT HE WAS A COACH THAT COACHES ENTERTAINING FOOTBALL. MY RELATIONSHIP (WITH LEACH) . . . IT WAS GOOD, BUT WE HAD THINGS WE DISAGREED ON AS WELL. IN FACT, I DON'T KNOW TOO MANY COACHES I'VE HAD THAT EVERYTHING HAS BEEN A 100 PERCENT EYE-TO-EYE."

— *Myers*, *October 24, 2009*

"I THINK THAT MIKE LEACH IS THE ABSOLUTE BEST COACH THAT TEXAS TECH HAS HAD, BECAUSE OF THE WAY HE PLAYS. YOU CAN'T PLAY IN THIS LEAGUE THE WAY OKLAHOMA AND TEXAS PLAY, AND MIKE DOESN'T DO THAT. HE WAS GOING TO DO SOMETHING DIFFERENT (AIR RAID OFFENSE). THAT'S WHAT HIS GAME WAS, AND IT WAS SO IDEALLY SUITED TO THIS SCHOOL IN THIS GEOGRAPHIC LOCATION IN TERMS OF RECRUITING THAT YOU COULD HAVE SPENT FIVE YEARS AND YOU WOULDN'T HAVE FOUND ANYBODY EQUAL TO LEACH AS A CHOICE. THE GUY THAT GETS THE CREDIT FOR MIKE BEING HERE — AND I KNOW WHAT HAPPENED WHEN MIKE WAS HIRED AND ALL THAT WAS INVOLVED — AND IF IT HAD NOT BEEN FOR GERALD MYERS, MIKE LEACH WOULD NOT BE COACHING HERE. IF YOU WERE TO HAVE A PICK OF THE CENTURY FOR AN ATHLETIC DIRECTOR, IT WOULD BE GERALD MYERS PICKING MIKE LEACH."

— *Bob Knight*, *on the ESPN Game Day set of the Texas at Texas Tech contest, November 2008*

"TECH'S (SUCCESSFUL 2008) SEASON STARTS BECAUSE GERALD MYERS HIRED LEACH. THAT'S THE MOST IMPORTANT THING TO THIS SEASON. THAT'S NO. 1 BECAUSE THEY WANTED TO HIRE (RICH) RODRIGUEZ, THE COMMITTEE DID, AND GERALD FOUGHT (BECAUSE) THEY WANTED TO START THE WHOLE SEARCH ALL OVER AGAIN. GERALD REALLY FOUGHT THAT AND HE WON, AND THEY HIRED LEACH."

— *Knight*

"I'M VERY SAD TO SAY THERE'S ONLY ONE PERSON TO BLAME FOR THIS AND IT'S MIKE LEACH. . . . I LIKE HIM AND I WANTED HIM TO BE MY COACH, BUT INSUBORDINATION AND THIS TYPE OF ACTIVITY JUST CANNOT BE PERMITTED."

— *Hance*, *after Leach's termination*

"HE'S NOT LIKE MOST COACHES. THE PEOPLE AT TEXAS TECH TOOK THAT PERSONALLY. THEY FELT SNUBBED AT TIMES. MIKE WASN'T DOING THAT DELIBERATELY. HE'S FROM CODY, WYOMING. HE'S A FOOTBALL COACH. HE'S NOT A HOBNOBBER, AND HE'S NOT AN ASS KISSER."

— *Gary O'Hagan*, *Leach's agent*

"THERE WAS A LONG CONTEXT BEHIND A LOT OF THE DIFFICULTIES AT TECH. OVER TIME, A LACK OF GOOD COMMUNICATION. WHEN THE PROBLEM AROSE, RATHER THAN BEING RESOLVED, IT JUST BLEW UP."

— *Guy Bailey*, *Texas Tech president, on the Leach situation*

"I THINK MIKE DID A GOOD JOB. WE WERE BETTER IN MANY AREAS, BUT I WANT A COACH WHO CAN BEAT TEXAS MORE THAN 20 PERCENT OF THE TIME. I THINK WE'RE A TOP 25 PROGRAM, AND I THINK WE WILL GET BETTER. LEACH NEVER TALKED ABOUT CHAMPIONSHIPS, BUT TUBERVILLE SAID THAT'S HIS GOAL."

— *Hance, on replacing Leach with Tommy Tuberville. For the record, Tuberville was 0-3 against Texas; never had the Red Raiders nationally ranked at the end of the season, and won no championships. He abruptly resigned after three seasons, with a 20-17 overall record and never posting a winning season in Big 12 play.*

"MIKE DID A GOOD JOB HERE; HE WON GAMES. BUT THE THING HERE IS THAT WE DON'T WANT TO TRY AND JUST WIN GAMES, WE WANT TO TRY AND WIN CHAMPIONSHIPS."

— *Tommy Tuberville*, *on taking the Texas Tech job*

"WE HAVE UPGRADED WITH A BETTER COACH, AND WE'RE GOING THROUGH SOME TOUGH TIMES RIGHT NOW. BUT WE HAVE THE UT-MOST CONFIDENCE IN HIM. HE'S A PROVEN WINNER, AND I THINK WE JUST HAVE TO HAVE PATIENCE TO BUILD THE PROGRAM THE WAY WE WANT IT TO BE."

— *Hance, on supporting Tuberville, who, in his first season, started 3-3*

"I HATED TO LEAVE TEXAS TECH. WE HAD SOME SUCCESS. IT WAS A HARD JOB BECAUSE I WAS TAKING OVER FOR KIND OF A LEGEND, A GUY WHO HAD TAKEN A PROGRAM THAT WAS DOWN AND OUT AND BUILT IT BACK. I WAS KIND OF THE OUTSIDER LOOKING IN FOR THREE YEARS. THAT HAD A LITTLE SOMETHING TO DO WITH IT, BUT THERE WERE GREAT PEOPLE THERE. IT WAS NICE. WE HAD BUILT THE PROGRAM BACK TO WHERE I THOUGHT IT WAS VERY COMPETITIVE, BUT THERE WAS ALWAYS IN THE BACK OF MY MIND, 'AM I EVER GOING TO WIN OVER THIS 25 TO 30 PERCENT THAT STILL LIKE MIKE?' RIGHT OR WRONG, IS THAT GOING TO HAPPEN? SOMETIMES YOU MAKE DECISIONS FOR THAT REASON. I'VE DONE ABOUT AS MUCH AS I CAN DO."

— ***Tommy Tuberville***, *on leaving Texas Tech for Cincinnati, 2013*

"I THINK IT'S A GREAT DAY FOR TEXAS TECH. WE HAVE SOMEONE THAT WANTS TO BE HERE AND THAT IS NOT GOING TO BE SHOPPING AROUND EVERY YEAR. I'VE KNOWN HIM ALL OF HIS LIFE. I COULD NOT BE HAPPIER. WHAT HAPPENED LAST SATURDAY (TUBERVILLE'S RESIGNATION) WAS A BLESSING IN DISGUISE, AND I FEEL BETTER ABOUT TEXAS TECH FOOTBALL THAN I'VE EVER FELT."

— ***Hance***, *on the hiring of Kliff Kingsbury*
after the sudden resignation of Tuberville, 2013

"I majored in American studies, and I've read about America for a long time. I have said the Pledge of Allegiance a lot and have studied the Constitution, and nothing in the material I've sifted through suggests that a state agency should be allowed to cheat somebody out of what they owe just because they're a state agency."

— ***Leach***, *on Tech's "sovereign immunity"*
defense in refusing to pay him

In ten seasons at Texas Tech, Mike Leach never had a losing record. He is the all-time winningest coach in school history with a record of 84-43.

"Which means virtually every coach at a (Texas) state institution is on a day-to-day contract. Kind of begs the question why we fought England, really."

— **Leach,** *on the sovereign immunity law in Texas, which he challenged and lost in court*

In retrospect, Leach might have been well advised to have researched the case of *Lemons v. Dodds*, University of Texas. Abe Lemons, the former UT basketball coach, was fired in 1982. He first sued athletic director DeLoss Dodds, and then followed that up later with a $2.3 million lawsuit against the University, claiming the school owed him for various fringe benefits which were lost when he was terminated. Lemons, who had two years remaining on his contract, charged in the suit that the university did not pay him for the loss of revenue from basketball camps, speaking engagements, a Nike shoe contract, and radio and television rights to his coach's show.

"Sovereign immunity" was cited as Lemons was unsuccessful in both cases.

In 1999, former UT baseball coach Cliff Gustafson filed suit against Dodds after Gustafson had been forced to resign in 1996. He, too, lost in court, with sovereign immunity, again, figuring into the decision. Prior to this ruling, Lemons offered his opinion of Gustafson's chances in the courtroom:

"He's got no chance. They've (UT) got lawyers who could get Hitler off. Plus, they've got those pre-lawyers paid for, and you've got to pay for yours."

Added Lemons:

"The school is the one that has the money. But you have to be slicker than a dandelion to get it."

"THEY DIDN'T ASK FOR IT, SO WE DIDN'T PRODUCE IT. . . . IT DOESN'T
SEEM TO ME THAT IT'S THAT BIG A DEAL. THEY'RE TRYING TO MAKE
EVERYTHING INTO A HUGE DEAL. NEXT, THEY'RE GOING TO SAY THAT
HANCE, MYERS, AND BAILEY WERE INVOLVED IN THE ASSASSINATION
OF PRESIDENT KENNEDY. THEY'RE GOING TO HAVE SOME DOCUMENT.
THIS IS JUST SO BIZARRE."

— *Dicky Grigg*, *Texas Tech attorney,*
on a request from Leach's counsel

"In the time I was there, we had three chancellors and five presidents.
That's eight altogether. Two of those chancellors were great, brilliant
men. One of them was a corrupt, power-hungry, jealous person that
wants all the attention directed at him and wants his own football
coach. . . . I got along with seven of eight over ten years. You do the
math, and you tell me what the problem is."

— *Leach*

"It was more of a 'respect everyone, fear no one' kind of mentality.
We were getting ready to explode and a lot of it had to do with the
connection between the community, our fans. Basically, there was
really good chemistry and I thought that helped our team, and other
than a handful of dubious characters that ended up in the administration, we were gonna win games and continue to win; there was no
question about that."

— *Leach*, *reflecting on his success at Texas Tech*

"Together, you don't accomplish anything unless you work together with the fans. I think what we did together, the players, coaches, fans, everybody, I thought was a big ten years, and then, obviously, there was a little corruption involved with my ousting. I think there are certain people at Tech who lost a lot of credibility over that. I think that all the fans want to be proud of their university. Keep in mind they haven't even paid me for 2009."

*— **Leach**, reflecting on his ouster from Tech*

"I'm looking for a school that wants to win football games, values graduation rates, and one where the efforts of all entities of the university are celebrated. When things were really rolling at Texas Tech, I was part of something bigger than football. You have an impact in a lot of ways, and you get to be a part of it and that's really thrilling. It affects a lot of people. It's gigantic."

*— **Leach***

"I would go with somebody that's committed to doing things in a team effort. Honestly, Tech was like that for the most part. . . . I'm not the only casualty. I'm the highest-profile casualty. We've got heads of departments, head of the medical school, head of the law school, we've got a lot of casualties there in some of the insanity and private agenda that goes on there, and I think a lot of that speaks for itself."

*— **Leach**, on his prospects for a new job*

"I THINK MIKE'S A GOOD COACH. I HOPE THAT HE MOVES ON WITH HIS LIFE. HE'S GOT A JOB NOW. I JUST WISH HIM THE BEST, BUT WE'VE MOVED ON A LONG TIME AGO."

— *Hance, after Leach became head coach at Washington State*

"I'm not a guy who fails to address things. The book was about my path to coaching and didn't stray from that, but we've got two chapters on the Tech aftermath. It does illustrate some of the devious things that go on behind the scenes with various individuals, and what makes those two chapters very powerful is the question of whether there are two sides to the story. Well, there aren't. There's one. We included an appendix with sworn statements, memos, receipts, records from the perpetrators, and that's written not in my words, not in [co-writer] Bruce Feldman's words — it's written in their words."

— *Leach, on two chapters in his 2011 book,*
Swing Your Sword, *detailing his ouster from Texas Tech*

"Their smear campaign has had a chilling effect, no question about it. I didn't have any choice except to set the record straight. What's powerful about those last chapters is that it's all out there, in the words of the perpetrators themselves. And they're embarrassed about what's out there."

— *Leach, on his book and his very public ouster from Tech*

"OF COURSE, THE BOOK IS MIKE'S SIDE OF WHAT HAPPENED, AND MIKE USES THE DOCUMENTS THAT SUPPORT HIS SIDE. REMEMBER, THERE ARE THOUSANDS OF COURT RECORDS AND DOCUMENTS. IF I WROTE THAT BOOK, I'D PRESENT MY SIDE AND I'D USE A DIFFERENT SET. SO, WHAT YOU HAVE TO REMEMBER, IF YOU READ THE BOOK,

YOU'RE READING A PARTICULAR SLANT AND THE DOCUMENTS CHOSEN ARE CHOSEN FOR THAT SLANT."

— *Guy Bailey*, *Texas Tech president*

"I UNDERSTAND MIKE HAS CHOSEN TO TAKE PERSONAL SHOTS AT ME AND OTHERS IN HIS BOOK, AND THAT'S UNFORTUNATE. I HAVE NOT READ THE BOOK AND HAVE NO INTENTION OF READING IT. I HAVE MOVED ON, AND SO HAS TEXAS TECH UNIVERSITY. MIKE KNOWS I WAS HIS BIGGEST FAN WHILE HE WAS HERE, BUT HIS POOR JUDGMENT AND HIS ACTIONS GAVE THE UNIVERSITY ADMINISTRATION NO CHOICE BUT TO TERMINATE HIM; AND ALTHOUGH WE DID EVERYTHING WE COULD TO ENCOURAGE MIKE TO HELP US RESOLVE THE SITUATION, I ULTIMATELY AGREED THAT THE RELATIONSHIP WAS DAMAGED BEYOND REPAIR."

— *Kent Hance*

"SOMEBODY WILL PROBABLY WRITE A REALLY GOOD BOOK ON THAT SITUATION ONE DAY, BUT NOT ANYTIME SOON. IT'S TOO BAD THINGS WORKED OUT THE WAY THEY DID. IT'S BETTER FOR MIKE TO GET A FRESH START SOMEWHERE ELSE, AND TECH NEEDED ONE, TOO."

— *Guy Bailey*, *Texas Tech president, reflecting on the Leach situation, shortly before leaving to become president at Alabama*

"You don't have much of that bureaucratic turf war stuff. Everybody pulls the same way. I think a lot of that has to do with the leadership here. That's where it's prevented. That's where the vision's set."

— *Leach*, *on his new job at Washington State and its administration, 2012*

"THE WORST (OFF-SEASON HIRE) WAS WASHINGTON STATE AND MIKE LEACH. THE WHEELS WERE COMING OFF FOR LEACH AT TEXAS TECH BEFORE HE WAS LET GO THERE. SET ASIDE THE ADAM JAMES ISSUE, WHETHER HE SAID, HE SAID, WHATEVER HAPPENS THERE. BUT I HAPPEN TO KNOW THAT HE COMPLETELY LOST CONTROL OF THAT PROGRAM. A LOT OF THE PLAYERS WONDERING WHAT WAS GOING ON. HE WAS LATE TO MEETINGS. HE OFTEN DIDN'T COME TO THE OFFICE UNTIL ONE OR TWO IN THE AFTERNOON. SO, I THINK MIKE LEACH'S TIME AS A HEAD COACH IS OVER, AND I THINK WASHINGTON STATE REALLY STRETCHED WITH THIS HIRE."

— ***Ed Cunningham***, *ESPN college football analyst*

"I REPRESENT THOUSANDS OF FOOTBALL COACHES WHO, NO MATTER WHERE MIKE LEACH WENT, WE WERE GOING TO PULL FOR HIM BECAUSE OF HOW HE GOT SCREWED AT TEXAS TECH, AND I MEAN THAT SINCERELY."

— ***Jim Walden***, *former Washington State coach, on Leach's hiring at WSU*

"HE'S NOW GOT A JOB — HE WENT TWO YEARS WITHOUT A JOB, AND I'M ALL FOR HIM HAVING THAT JOB AT WASHINGTON STATE. THAT WAY, HE'S NOT SITTING AROUND MESSING WITH US THE WHOLE TIME. BUT I WISH HIM THE BEST AND HOPE HE LEARNED FROM WHAT HAPPENED AT TEXAS TECH."

— ***Hance***, *2014*

18
Fun in the Sun and Snow with the Hurricanes

"Mike Leach and his entire staff have done a tremendous job in building our football program, and the goal is to keep moving forward. Cougar football has returned to the upper echelon of collegiate football where it most deservedly belongs. I believe I speak for all Cougar fans when I say we want Mike Leach leading our football program for many years to come."

— **Bill Moos**, Washington State athletic director, on extending Leach's contract through 2020, December 29, 2015

While many thought the hiring of Mike Leach would bring instant success to a downtrodden Cougar program, the team struggled to a 3-9 record in 2012. A season-ending upset of Apple Cup rival Washington did offer some optimism for 2013.

The coach's demanding work ethic and calling out of players ruffled some feathers within the ranks that first year. One talented wide receiver left the team in mid-season, claiming that players were being abused by the coaching staff. Subsequent investigations by the school and Pac-12 uncovered no such abuses.

By year two of the Leach era, things had settled down. The Cougars began to turn the corner, even while playing one of the nation's toughest schedules. In 2013, Washington State defeated such Pac-12 foes as Southern Cal and Arizona en route to a 6-6 record. That earned the Cougars their first bowl bid in ten years — the New Mexico Bowl.

After jumping on Colorado State early, Washington State had a late-game meltdown to lose the post-season contest. But the future appeared bright, as record-setting quarterback Connor Halliday would be returning in 2014, to be joined by a host of talented recruits.

But the Cougars stumbled out of the gate in 2014, opening the season with back-to-back upset losses to Rutgers and Nevada. A win over previously undefeated and nationally ranked Utah briefly righted the ship. But the next week, with a chance to even their record at 3-3, the Cougars experienced a devastating 60-59 loss to California, missing an eighteen-yard game-winning field goal attempt on the final play of the game. Washington State lost five of its last six games, and Halliday went down with a season-ending leg injury against USC in week nine. As might be expected, as the losses and frustration mounted, the coach's weekly press conferences became more contentious.

So it was another 3-9 season — eight of the losses were to teams who earned bowl invitations, including a 38-31 loss to national title runner-up Oregon — and a disappointing three-year mark of 12-25 for Leach and company.

Immediately after a season-ending Apple Cup loss to Washington, Leach dismissed both his defensive coordinator and linebackers coach. Earlier in the season, after an abysmal performance by the Wazzu special teams, the special teams coach was fired.

Not surprisingly, after three disappointing seasons, Leach and the Cougars didn't receive much pre-season hype in 2015. In fact, most pundits picked the Cougs to finish near the bottom of the Pac-12 standings.

Unfortunately, Wazzu lived up to its pre-season billing in its season opener with an embarrassing 24-17 loss at home to Portland State — an FCS team. In the process, the home team blew a 10-0, second-quarter lead.

Alumni and fans were outraged, with many wanting to examine the possibility of buying out the coach's contract.

The Cougars next limped into Piscataway, New Jersey, to take on Rutgers. Looking face-to-face at a second disastrous loss, the Cougars somehow pulled out a 37-34 victory. The game-winner came on an eight-yard pass from standout sophomore quarterback Luke Falk to

River Cracraft with just thirteen seconds left.

After splitting its next two games (beating Wyoming, 31-14, and losing to California, 34-28) WSU worked its magic again at Oregon.

The Cougars came from behind to tie the game with one second remaining on a pass from Falk to Dom Williams and then defeated the Ducks in double overtime, 45-38.

After wins over Oregon State and Arizona State ran their record to 5-2, the Cougars hosted eighth-ranked Stanford. On a rainy night in Pullman, Erik Powell kicked five field goals, but missed a forty-three-yard attempt on the final play of the game as WSU fell, 30-28.

Washington State rebounded to win its next three games, including another last-second thriller over nineteenth-ranked UCLA. This time, Falk tossed a twenty-one-yard scoring strike to Gabe Marks with three seconds remaining to give WSU a 31-27 victory.

Falk suffered a concussion the next week in a 27-3 win over Colorado. He then missed the Apple Cup game against rival Washington, and the nineteenth-ranked Cougs lost, 45-10.

After finishing the season 8-4 and third in the Pac-12 North (6-3, behind Stanford and Oregon), Washington State received a bid to the Sun Bowl in El Paso, Texas.

The Cougars held on to defeat the Miami (Fla). Hurricanes, 20-14, in a late December snowstorm. It marked the program's first bowl victory (and most wins) since 2003.

For his efforts in 2015, Leach was named Pac-12 Co-Coach of the Year, along with David Shaw of Stanford. Shortly thereafter, WSU athletic director Bill Moos added a year to the coach's contract, extending it through the 2020 season.

Sources/Further Reading

Newspapers

Abilene Reporter-News / reporternews.com
Amarillo Globe-News / amarillo.com
Arizona Republic / azcentral.com
Austin American-Statesman / statesman.com
Baltimore Sun / baltimoresun.com
Bryan Eagle / theeagle.com
Cedar Rapids Gazette / thegazette.com
The Columbian (Washington) / Columbian.com
The Daily (Washington) *Evergreen* / dailyevergreen.com
The Daily Toreador / dailytoreador.com
The Dallas Morning News / dallasnews.com
The Dallas Observer / dallasobserver.com
Denver Post / denverpost.com
El Paso Times / elpasotimes.com
Fort Worth Star-Telegram / star-telegram.com
Houston Chronicle / chronicle.com
Kansas City Star / kansascity.com
Kerrville Daily Times / dailytimes.com
Kitsap (Washington) *Sun* / kitsapsun.com
Lexington (Kentucky) *Herald-Leader* / kentucky.com
Los Angeles Times / latimes.com
Lubbock Avalanche-Journal / lubbockonline.com
Midland Reporter-Telegram / mrt.com
Montgomery (Alabama) *Advertiser* / montgomeryadvertiser.com
New York Times / nytimes.com
The Oklahoman / newsok.com
Orange (Texas) *Leader* / orangeleader.com
The Oregonian / oregonlive.com
Paris (Texas) *News* / theparisnews.com

Plainview (Texas) *Herald* / myplainview.com
The Press (Calif.) *Enterprise*
Richmond Times-Dispatch / richmond.com
San Diego Union Tribune / utsandiego.com
Salt Lake Tribune / sltrib.com
San Antonio Express-News / mysanantonio.com
Seattle Times / seattletimes.com
The Spokesman-Review / spokesman.com
The Topeka Capital-Journal / cjonline.com
Tulsa World / tulsaworld.com
University Daily (changed to *The Daily Toreador*, Texas Tech's student
    newspaper, in 2005)
USA Today / usatoday.com
Waco Tribune-Herald / wacotrib.com
The Wall Street Journal / wsj.com
Washington Post / washingtonpost.com
Waterloo-Cedar Falls Courier / wcfcourier.com

Newsletters
The Fifth Down, Football Writers Association of America

Magazines
American Football Monthly
ESPN The Magazine
Lubbock Magazine
Men's Journal
New York Times Magazine
Sports Illustrated
Texas Lawyer
Texas Monthly
Texas Techsan alumni magazine

Media Guides

Texas Tech football
University of Texas basketball

Books

Benedict, Jeff, and Armen Keteyian. *The System: The Glory and Scandal of Big-time College Football.* Doubleday, 2013.

Brown, Chris B. *The Essential Smart Football.* SCBB Press. 2012.

Burton, Alan. *Pirates, Soldiers & Fat Little Girlfriends: More Classic Texas Sports Quotes.* Zone Press, 2010.

Davidson, James E., and Ralph L. Sellmeyer. *The Red Raiders: Texas Tech Football.* Strode Publishers, 1978.

Didinger, Ray, and Glen Macnow. *The Ultimate Book of Sports Movies: Featuring the 100 Greatest Sports Films of All Time.* Running Press, 2009.

Dykes, Spike, with Dave Boling. *Spike Dykes's Tales from the Texas Tech Sideline.* Sports Publishing LLC, 2004.

Feldman, Bruce, and Mike Leach. *Swing Your Sword: Leading the Charge in Football and Life.* Diversion Books, 2011.

Guven, Ferhat, and Mike Leach. *Sports for Dorks: College Football.* Sports Dorks CFB, LLC, 2011.

Heard, Robert. *You Scored One More Point Than a Dead Man: The Irresistible, Sardonic Humor of Abe Lemons.* Austin, Texas: Lemons-Heard Company, 1978.

Kiser, Rob. *Stretch the Cornfield.* State House Press, 2013.

Klosterman, Chuck. *Eating the Dinosaur.* Scribner, New York, 2009.

Koppett, Leonard. *The Rise and Fall of the Press Box.* Sports Media, Toronto, 2003.

Koppett, Leonard. *Sports Illusion, Sports Reality: A Reporter's View of Sports, Journalism and Society.* Houghton Mifflin, Boston, 1981.

Lanning, Michael Lee. *Double T – Double Cross: The Firing of Mike Leach.* Scottsdale Book Publishing, 2011.

Leach, Mike, and Buddy Levy. *Geronimo: Leadership Strategies of an American Warrior*. Gallery Books, 2014.

McMinn, Ed. *Texas Tech Daily Devotions for Die-Hard Fans*. Extra Point Publishers, Perry, Georgia, 2013.

Royal, Darrell, with Blackie Sherrod. *Darrell Royal Talks Football*. Prentice Hall, 1963.

Shipps, Anthony. *The Quote Sleuth: A Manual for the Tracer of Lost Quotations*. The University of Illinois Press, 1990.

Smith, Dean O., *Understanding Authority in Higher Education*. Rowman and Littlefield, 2015.

Spector, Stephen. *May I Quote You On That? A Guide to Grammar and Usage*. Oxford University Press, New York, 2015.

Walden, Jim, Dave Boling, and Bud Withers. *Tales from the Washington State Cougars Sideline: A Collection of the Greatest Cougars Stories Ever Told*. Sports Publishing, 2013.

Weinreb, Michael. *Season of Saturdays: A History of College Football in 14 Games*. Scribner, New York, 2014.

Wright, Bart. *Football Revolution: The Rise of the Spread Offense and How It Transformed College Football*. University of Nebraska Press, 2013.

TV

CBS College Sports Network
CBS *60 Minutes*
ESPN halftime, post-game
ESPN *College Game Day*
ESPN *Sportscenter*
ESPN *First Take*
ESPNU
FX TV
Fox Sports Southwest
Fox Sports Ohio
Friday Night Lights

Jimmy Kimmel Live!
KAMC TV Lubbock
KOCO TV Oklahoma City
KXLY Spokane
NBC *Tonight Show with Jay Leno*
Pac-12 Network
Texas Tribune

Radio

The Zone 1300 AM, Austin, Texas
KESN/103.3 FM ESPN, Dallas-Fort Worth
KGA Sports Radio 1510 AM, Spokane, Washington
KIRO 710 AM ESPN, Seattle, Washington
ESPN 104.5 FM, Albany, New York
The Fan 105.3 FM, Dallas-Fort Worth
KHYI 95.3 FM, Texas Tech radio network post-game interviews, Howe,
Texas
KRLD 1080 AM, Dallas, Texas
KXL 101 FM, Portland, Oregon
102.9 FM, The Bald Faced Truth, Portland, Oregon
KXTG 750 AM, Portland, Oregon
SiriusXM College Sports Nation
Sports Talk Bo Mattingly Sportstalkwithbo.com Arkansas
Sportsradio 1310 AM, The Ticket, Dallas, Texas
WCCP 104.9 FM, Clemson, South Carolina
WJOX 94.5 FM Birmingham, Alabama
WBAP 820 AM, Fort Worth, Texas
ESPN 104.5 FM, Baton Rouge, Louisiana

Websites

aggiesports.com
allcougdup.com
asapsports.com

baylorfans.com
big12sports.com
bitterlawyer.com
cbssports.com
coachingsearch.com
cougcenter.com
cougfan.com
cyinterview.com
dailypress.com
espn.go.com
footballrecruiting.rivals.com
foxnews.com
foxsports.com
hailvarsity.com
jimmoorethegotoguy.com
kusports.com
larrybrownsports.com
lifeinlubbock.com
pacifictakes.com
reddit.com
redraiders.com
redraidersports.com
rgj.com
rivals.comcollegefootball
seattlepi.com
sbnation.com
si.com
sportsbybrooks.com
sportsonearth.com
sportstalkwithbo.com
texastech.com
texastechscout.com
thegazette.com
vivathematadors.com

wikipedia.com
wreckemred.com
wsucougars.com
yahoosports.com

Videos

George Munger Coach of the Year banquet
Big 12 Media Day 2009
Texas Tech athletics
Washington State athletics
Spokesman-Review videos

Other

Associated Press
CSTV U-wire

About the Author

Alan Burton

Throughout his thirty-year writing career, Alan Burton has been honored by such organizations as the Associated Press, Texas School Public Relations Association, and Oklahoma College Public Relations Association.

A native of Sherman, Texas, Burton is the author of six books.

He has thirty-three years of media/communications experience, and has served in various capacities in the field of educational public relations for the past twenty-seven years.

Burton is a 1979 graduate of Texas Tech University, where he earned a bachelor of arts in English. He currently serves as Special Assistant to the president/director of university communications at Southeastern Oklahoma State University. He was director of community relations for the Sherman Independent School District from 1988-99.

Other books by Alan Burton

Til the fat lady sings . . . Classic Texas Sports Quotes, Texas Tech University Press, 1994

Rave On . . . Classic Texas Music Quotes, Texas Tech University Press, 1996

Texas High School Hotshots, Republic of Texas Press, 2002

Dallas Cowboys Quips and Quotes, State House Press, 2006

Pirates, Soldiers & Fat Little Girlfriends...More Classic Texas Sports Quotes, Zone Press, 2010